Stock Investing Fundamentals

Simplicity is the Ultimate in Sophisticated Investing

R. Stewart Eads, CFA

ISBN-13: 978-1453744802

Contents

Chapter 1: Introduction

This series of articles will put forth some rather profound concepts that may well have a dramatic effect on equity investing as we know it. For starters there are three, and only three, components for the total investment return of any stock over any period of time. They are:

- Growth rate of earnings per share (percent per year)
- Dividend yield (percent per year)
- Change in the price to earnings (PE) ratio (percent per year)

Ultimately (say, over 30 years), stock prices go where earnings go. However, over the shorter term, PE changes can deflect the strict adherence of a stock price to its earnings growth. It will be argued that it is inflation, not interest rates, that serves as a key determinant of the long-term trend in stock PE ratios. That is, inflation is a discount rate for valuing the discounted present value of a future stream of corporate earnings. A stock price at any point in time is simply the discounted present value of future earnings per share. When investors are optimistic they tend to look out further in discounting. When they are pessimistic they look out less far. The belief in using inflation as the discount rate is based on a long history of empirical evidence (approximately 100 years worth). However, using inflation as the discount rate instead of interest rates is in direct contrast to conventional Wall Street wisdom. The other key long-term determinant of where stock prices go is, of course, the earnings growth rates.

It will be argued that a complete investment cycle in the U.S. has tended to be approximately 30 years in length. Linked to these concepts, it will be argued that it is possible to discern when one should focus on growth stocks and when one should focus on value stocks. It will be argued that the Standard & Poor's 500 stock index fund could be considered a cop-out for those investors without a clue as to what is going on in secular long-term style shifts between growth stocks and value stocks.

A "growth" stock investor in the 1972 to 1987 time period generally had poor returns when compared to investors in "value" stocks. More on the definitions of "growth" and "value" later.

The point will be made that the approximate 10% long-term (30 years) average annual compound rate of return for the U.S. stock market is made up of long periods where the market tended to average returns much better that 10% and long periods where it averaged returns much less than 10%. All of the above has very important implications for personal retirement planning models as well as for investing in general. Applicability of the ideas contained herein should run the gamut from the small individual investor up to the giant corporate retirement plan and college endowment.

By no means are these articles meant to be some sort of get rich quick scheme or to give the impression that successful long-term investing is easy. The intent herein is to help focus your attention on:

1.   Setting your long-term investment objectives to include both absolute and relative (to inflation, the overall stock market, etc.) return goals, risk tolerance and time horizons. Any special income needs or other special constraints should be included.

2.   Outlining Future Investment Themes that you believe could have investment significance over the next five years.

3.   Forecasting the future rate of consumer price inflation.

4.   Forecasting the future earnings/share growth rates for the Standard & Poor's 500 stock index and individual companies in which you will consider investing.

5.   Forecasting the trend of the price/earnings ratio for the Standard & Poor's 500 stock Index and for companies in which you might invest.

In buying common stocks it is good to have as much going for you as possible. That is, as much as possible, use stocks with a good long-term record of earnings growing at a steady, consistent and healthy rate. As a general rule, stay away from new issues and turn-around situations. Stick with proven long-term consistent winners. Also, owning good stocks that you believe are riding a good Future Theme is advisable. Devising useful Future Themes is tricky, however. It is useful to reflect back on so-called themes that never worked out. Years ago, the oceans were going to be tapped for bountiful riches. Several decades later, this has not worked out as predicted other than maybe oil drilling.

Not to oversimplify, if you could predict the future earnings and dividend growth rates for a stock and gauge the trend in inflation (and thus price/earnings ratios) over the next several years, you would have what you need to determine your expected rate of return. If your time horizon was 30-35 years, the PE prediction would likely not be vital since the PE effect would have had a complete cycle and the stock price would probably follow the earnings growth.

There are a multitude of books out on investing in stocks and bonds. What could there be left to say? The focus here is on rudimentary concepts to help the investor have a much better understanding of the key determinants of stock price valuations over the long-term future. Much reliance is based on what empirical history has to teach us combined with logical ideas of why stock prices have done what they have done over time. The concepts expressed herein can be understood by anyone willing to take the time to reflect on them. There are no higher mathematics involved. Still, the concepts are profound.

Reading and understanding the ideas here will likely place you in the upper percentile of all investors in regards to understanding the stock market. You may even find you have a better understanding of the long-term workings of the stock market than your current financial advisors. The emphasis in these articles will be on "trends" -- thus, you will see the repeated use of ten year averages of data series. This is done to focus on longer-term trends and not year-to-year noise on which no one can predict or gain an advantage. It is riding the right trends in the overall stock market and in individual stocks that can make one very wealthy. Attempting to play the near-term gyrations in stock prices is generally a fool's game. An advisor might have recommended that you take your profit in Wal-Mart in the 1970's after you had doubled your money. "You can't argue with taking a profit". But, if you had held the stock for 35 years…wow!

U. S. equity investors are subjected to an overload of information, much of which is not productive for long-term investment success. The purpose of these articles is to discuss some rather simple concepts that are borne out in history and common sense. These concepts will not provide a certain road to riches in equity investing, but will allow one to focus energies on those endeavors that will be the most productive in the pursuit of success through equity investing. Some of the ideas put forth herein are rather profound and may well have a dramatic impact on equity investing as we currently know it.

This series of articles on investing will likely have very limited appeal for several reasons as follows:

- The focus is not about a coming worldwide economic debacle. Books on economic gloom and doom do very well. Query why?
- The articles are not a glib, easy to read treatise on how to make a quick killing by "playing the stock market." The shelves at leading bookstores are already full of such books.
- The articles address a multitude of boring topics such as setting your long-term investment objectives, historical rates of return from investing in stocks, bonds and other investments, which investment style to select and other fundamentals important for success.

The items addressed herein are simply not what sells books to the masses. The purpose here is to appeal to the limited audience of intelligent, thinking investors -- the type investors not easily separated from their money.

The articles are somewhat of a maverick in that they are not about arcane academic theories at the one extreme, nor are they shallow and frivolous at the other extreme. They obtain a lot of their basis from empirical history and are very heavy on applied common sense gleaned from forty years in the investment business. Investment geeks are not cool. Colorful, loud talking prophets are fun to watch.

Beginning in the late 1970's I began predicting that the big news in the decade of the 1980's would be a dramatic drop in the high rate of inflation we had seen throughout much of the 1970's. Further, I predicted that this would cause the price/earnings ratio for common stocks to expand for the period 1980 on into the 1990's. I predicted that the average annual rate of return from investing in stocks from the early 1980's to the mid-1990's would be in the vicinity of 18-20% per year. This was very close to the actual results. My then associates at Wellington Management Company, and anyone I could get to listen, heard all of these predictions ad nauseam.

Citing the above is not to glorify myself, but only to make a very important point. Much of the fame and fortune made by some people on Wall Street often has nothing to do with making correct predictions or actually making money for clients. Unfortunately, as we have all learned over the past few years, some fame and fortune on Wall Street is garnered by going outside the law. Other fortunes are made by people in the business who are aggressive, charismatic salesmen -- actual investment results for clients often has very little to do with it. There are economists, strategists, market technicians and others who can pack ballrooms full of eager listeners even though their long-term forecasting records may be abysmal. Being a great speaker with charisma can sometimes overcome the annoying small stuff. Oftentimes, it is not even clear what their long-term record has been. How do you track the successes/failures of a stock market technician? Who measures their performance record? Who measures the performance record for an economist or for a stock market strategist? Who measures the investment success of brokers at the large stock brokerage firms?

Chapter 2: Simplicity and the Big Picture

We are all products of our upbringing, experience and environment. While working as a summer intern at NASA's George C. Marshall Space Flight Center during the summers of 1964 and 1965, I had several contacts with the Center's director, Dr. Wernher von Braun. He was one of the German rocket scientists sent to the United States at the end of World War II as lands and scientific talent were being divided up between the U.S. and the U.S.S.R. To my mind, the charismatic Dr. von Braun was the key individual behind the United States' success in putting a man on the moon by 1969. The entire Marshall Center exuded his confidence in the halcyon days of the 1960's.

One of Dr. von Braun's beliefs that made a lifelong impression on me was that "simplicity is the ultimate in sophistication." While his Saturn class rockets had complicated intricacies by necessity of the task at hand, the overall concept of the three-stage rocket with gimbaled (movable) engines was quite simple and profound. The mark of true intelligence and an understanding of a matter is being able to distill it down to the primary rudimentary factors and then explain it so that most people can understand what is being said. In many facets of life, people simply do not have a good foundation and understanding of what they are attempting to explain. That is often why they cannot present it clearly.

If you think about it, almost anyone can make a problem more complicated than it needs to be. Some people complicate things because they truly know no better -- they then become part of the problem they are trying to solve. Other people seem to purposely complicate problems so as to glorify their contributions to solving such a complex matter. It is a special skill to be able to distill a complex issue down to the key necessary components and discard all extraneous factors.

Regarding Wall Street wisdom, I firmly believe that history has a lot to teach us in order to best prepare us to predict the future. "Empirical analysis" is a good term to describe the process. This is not to be confused with so-called "technical analysis." History presents several dramatic relationships between key variables that are essential to examine in any rational attempt to predict the future for, say, the stock market.

After receiving my M.B.A. at Wharton, I spent the next three years in the Office of the Director of the U.S. Central Intelligence Agency in Langley, Virginia. Among other myriad tasks and assignments, I was given a satellite. More specifically, I was asked to do a systematic study of the data collected by this particular electronics satellite. My satellite did not take pictures. Its mission was to collect electronic signals from USSR radar. I created a computer model of "normal" ambient electronic signals by radar type and even tracked deviation from this norm. In the late 1960's, the U.S. was very interested in the Anti-Ballistic Missile (ABM) capabilities of the U.S.S.R. to better gauge how rapidly we needed to build our own ABM system. The U.S. was very interested in signals emitted by various U.S.S.R. radar installations believed to be integral to their ABM system. Intelligence on these Soviet ABM systems (actually, the lack of any such systems) eventually supported President Reagan's Star Wars bluff. This was one key factor in the ultimate downfall of the U.S.S.R. They simply could not afford to build a sophisticated ABM system.

My satellite had an expected life of three months and encircled the earth at approximately 100 miles altitude and had a collection swath of a few hundred miles across the earth. It flew at a northernmost latitude of approximately 80 degrees. It completed each trip around the world every 1.5 hours and made about 16 circles around the globe a day. This satellite, while it flew across virtually all of the U.S.S.R. over its life span, always tended to fly over the U.S.S.R. at approximately the same two times each day over its three months life. It sampled a lot of the terrain, but it sampled very little in the way of different times of the day. This phenomenon is simply governed by the relative position of a satellite's track relative to the sun. After all, position on the earth relative to the sun is what determines the time of day. Data sampling at different times of the day were dependent on the earth moving around the sun and the fact that the orbit precessed (moved) albeit slowly in galactic space because the orbit latitude was other than 90 degrees. In short, this satellite accomplished only a portion of round the clock local time sampling of the U.S.S.R. terrain, and it seemed that very few people realized this. Myriad details had been covered, but the understanding of the bigger picture key to the success of the mission seemed to be lacking. I presented the conclusions of my study to a packed room of admirals, generals and others in a basement conference room in the Pentagon in the late 1960's.

If you carefully read (and, possibly, reread) these articles and understand what you read, you will likely be in the top few percentile of people who understand the workings of the overall stock market and common stocks in general. You will be much better informed on what variables you should focus your attention on, what investment time frame makes sense and how to go about putting a rational investment program into place.

If we have discovered some basic truths of securities investing and tell all we know, does that not put us out of business? Quite the contrary, our best prospective clients are well educated in the realistic process of creating wealth using common stocks so they can avoid myriad advisors pursuing false horizons. In the final analysis, our best long-term clients are very successful people who understand the rudiments of successful long-term investing but simply do not want to tend to the nuts and bolts of day-to-day information gathering and following the successes and failures of numerous securities. They are simply too busy making money in other endeavors or have no interest in portfolio management. Further, they realize that successful stockbrokers are generally "salesmen" by necessity (gathering assets) and not analytical portfolio managers. They want someone who is totally focused on growing assets using prudent investment vehicles.

Chapter 3: The Guru Syndrome

The ability to peer into the future has long captivated humankind. It is tantamount to being able to foresee and control one's destiny. Whether in politics, economics, business, social structure, the stock market, or whatever, the ability to forecast major future trends gives one a significant advantage over one's competition. As it turns out, however, not many people are very good at this very difficult task. Still, whenever society perceives that it has discovered a seer, sage, oracle, or whatever term is preferred, it elevates that person to a pedestal and appoints them "guru." This has happened since ancient times.

Delphi, Greece is a rugged and beautiful area of mountains and valleys approximately 160 kilometers west of Athens. The natural features of the area lend to the historically sacred and mysterious character of the setting. In ancient times, the Oracle of Delphi was the most famous oracle in all of Greece. Those who wished to consult the oracle would first sacrifice a goat, sheep or other animal and then await their turn for a consultation. They would hand in questions written on leaden tablets. The priestess was an older peasant woman who, after purifying herself in the Castalian Fountain, drinking a special water and eating a laurel leaf, took a seat over a chasm to inhale intoxicating vapors that were exhaled from the chasm. Once intoxicated, she would utter incoherent sounds which were interpreted by the priests of Delphi and put into writing. The interpretations, which were always vague and equivocal, were given to the inquirer, who generally departed more confused than when he had arrived.

The Oracle of Delphi (per a babbling, intoxicated peasant woman) would at times decide the fate of nations regarding war, peace, national economics or other monumental events in Greece. Over 2000 years later, some things haven't changed at all. We have mystics who interpret stock market wave theories for mere mortals who cannot begin to understand the concepts involved. One is often reminded that, in the laws of probability, it is perfectly possible to flip, say, 20 consecutive heads in tossing a coin. It doesn't require skill -- merely the odds temporarily shifting that way. Also, one is reminded about the old saw that if you give a million monkeys each a typewriter, one may type a Shakespeare sonnet.

Similarly, if you have a large number of prospective stock market "gurus" making predictions week by week, month by month over several years, certainly one, or several, will end up with a good track record. The question is whether it was luck or skill. Being that analytical is no fun. It is a human tendency to anoint the winner "guru" and then proceed to follow their every utterance over the next several years -- often with poor results.

Being a stock market guru is no different than most things in life. The guru must have some record of accurate forecasting. (Often even a rather short record will do.) However, equally or more important, the person must generally be very intelligent (IQ wise), have excellent writing and/or speaking ability, ideally be a very colorful, exciting, flamboyant individual, and being physically attractive does not hurt at all. It helps a lot if the individual has an ability to coin cute, colorful and memorable phrases. The high IQ and verbal skills are very important here. The media is always hungry to find one or several gurus to interview and quote. So "once a guru, always a guru." That is, the media is not hung up so much on forecasting ability as it is on citing really colorful people who help sell newspapers or garner a TV audience. There are stock market gurus who made their reputations in the 1970's, were totally wrong in the 1980's (the lucky coin or monkey syndrome) and are still termed "guru" by the media. Some things will never change. Wouldn't life be dull if we couldn't have some fun?

Being a good forecaster of future events is not a natural by-product of having high intelligence any more than being a "creative" person is related to one's academic intellect. You are about as likely to find an oracle to predict future general trends in the world who is plowing a field in Georgia as wearing a three piece suit on Wall Street. It has to do with raw common sense and an ability to extrapolate history with a certain amount of unfettered realism tossed in.

As a matter of possible interest, some years ago the Air Force funded RAND Corporation work on a Delphi forecasting methodology. Simply stated, you select the most knowledgeable people on a topic of interest and ask them written questions requiring written responses. All answers are confidential regarding who says what, but the "first round" results are compiled and distributed to all participants who are then able to see where their opinions stand vis-a-vis their peers. They are then given a second chance to respond to the questions. Several iterations, with feedback each time, are used to arrive at stable best opinions. By using responses without names attached personalities, power and who has the loudest voice are left out of the equation. The search is for the best possible answers from the best possible people with a minimum weight given to extraneous factors.

A long-term survivor guru will often go into a career protection mode once his reputation is made. Although "once a guru, always a guru," some will become very middle of the road and bland in their predictions once their reputations are made. Gurus anointed by the media tend to be perpetuated if, for whatever reason, they are popular with customers. This is all not dissimilar from the advice given by the Oracle of Delphi.

Chapter 4: Investors Always Fight the Last Battle

Investors are first and foremost, living, breathing and emotional human beings. Generally, they are skeptical and rather cynical. At times they can become extremely euphoric and greedy while at other times they are very fearful. The extremes of stock market emotion are "euphoria" and "despair." During euphoria, everything is going well and, seemingly can never go wrong again. However, during despair nothing is going right and there is little chance that the market will ever be healthy again -- at least not within any meaningful time frame. There are just too many long-term problems around.

The stock market is an upward meandering beast that fluctuates between euphoria and despair as it meanders upward over the very long term. Investors tend to believe that whatever major dynamic currently prevails (good or bad) it will likely be around for a very long time. Even when a trend change (for the better or worse) does occur, investors tend to see the change as only sporadic and believe that the major underlying fundamentals will not change. For example, even as inflation steadily moved upward from the mid-1960's, investors kept investing as if inflation was still non-existent. This expectation of continued low inflation continued until the OPEC oil embargo hit in the fall of 1973 and left no doubt that inflation was a problem. Conversely, the OPEC group began to fall apart in the early 1980's, and as other inflationary forces had largely expended themselves, inflation dropped markedly. However, many economists and investors continued to expect inflation to come roaring back because of the huge federal budget deficits.

As a general rule, investors seem to have a tendency to not accept a major structural change until 5-7 years after the true inflection point. This is a good working assumption as it pertains to various models and procedures throughout these articles.

In investing, simple truths are always very valuable. Convoluted and complicated theories are usually wrong. One simple truth, as stated above, is that investors always tend to extrapolate history or, in other words, continue to fight the last battle. Dramatically increasing oil prices left no doubt about the direction of inflation. Although Growth stocks benefited much more than Value stocks from declining inflation, Growth stocks did not become the preferred equity style until approximately the end of 1988 when investors were finally able to accept that high inflation was gone....at least for a time.

To summarize, a good rule of thumb might be that investors tend to extrapolate a major trend event for 5-7 years after it has actually ended. However, to be smarter than the masses (i.e., early) can result in several years of investment frustration. Probably, the best advice is to realize that most investors will stick with an old trend far too long and act accordingly.

Chapter 5: The Efficient Market

Over the years much has been written about the efficiency of the U.S. stock market. Simply stated, this means that it is very difficult to perform better than a broad stock market index over a meaningful period of time since information is disseminated very quickly and all investors are investing based on the same information. The Standard & Poor's 500 stock index (S&P500) is a reasonable index to have in mind. In this series of articles whenever we refer to the "stock market" we will be referring to the S&P 500 index. We use Cowles Commission Stocks prior to 1926 as its proxy.

Belief in the Efficient Market causes some people to opt to invest in an index fund and forego "active" management. An index fund is simply a fund that mimics a popular stock market index....such as the S&P500 index. This is fine since a broad stock market index such as the S&P500 has historically returned approximately 10 percent per year on average over the long term. That is certainly a decent return.

If everyone simply bought an index fund, there would not be a steady reallocation of funds to the prospectively best future companies so far as society's best interests. In short, good companies would not be rewarded with ready financing to carry on their good work. However, the primary motivation of the individual investor is not to perform a public service regarding financing.

The more germane matter is the prospect of better returns than will be provided by an index fund over the long term. If one were able to beat an index fund by, say, two percent per year on average over 25 years that would add 64 percent to the return (not considering taxes). Of course, for a tax sheltered retirement fund there would be no taxes along the way. Two percent per year does not sound like much until compounding over a number of years takes place. Two percent per year additional return above an index fund is enough to be very meaningful but not so much as to meaningfully increase the amount of additional risk taken.

It is important to address the topic of risk. The Efficient Market thesis does come into play in regards to risk and return. Generally, there is no so-called free lunch in stock investing......or any investing for that matter. That is, risk tends to go hand-in-hand with prospective return. There are simply too many bright, well-informed and greedy investors to break the bond between risk and return. Think of it as a Mother Nature that watches over investing. One rule is that if you seek higher returns you are inherently taking on more risk. Risk matters when the bad times come and one can have a catastrophic loss in asset value. There are those who will then scream "foul" and "the system is rigged".

All of this might make one wonder how something called a hedge fund can defy the laws of risk and return. Certainly, they are managed by well-informed, bright and greedy people. Just keep in mind that higher returns simply do not come without commensurate risk having been taken. How could it be otherwise?

What about the claims that one cannot beat the "efficient" market in investing? If the efficiency of the market was total, it would also work against the success of individual company success stories. That is, companies such as Wal-Mart, Home Depot, Cisco, IBM, Procter & Gamble, Pepsico and myriad others would not be able to emerge as leaders. They surely deal with the same array of issues as do individual stock investors such as the rapid flow of information to bright and greedy competitors. While many competitors had the same information, they were not able to use it in the same well-organized, consistent manner and make a lot of good decisions along the way.

Many individual investors and professional investment firms have good information, bright people and certainly want to succeed. However, they may not make the best and most efficient use of their information by integrating it into a system that focuses on the few key variables and using the "noise" information to a much lesser degree. It truly takes a special kind of intellect and experience to sort out the big picture items that will allow one to potentially capture, say, the two percent per year return over a stock index fund. On the surface, all professionals may sound the same as they speak an arcane language. It is difficult to cut through to the ones who have a real handle on what they are doing.

Chapter 6: The Three Components of Equity Total Return

When you purchase a stock your total return will come from three and only three components. The first component is the earnings growth rate. Ultimately, a stock price will go where the earnings go. The second component of your total return is the change (percent per year) in the PE of the stock over the period of interest. The PE is the valuation placed on corporate earnings. The third, and final, component of your total return is the dividend yield (this is the dividends in dollars per share divided by the stock price per share and put into percentage terms).

The accompanying Chart 1 shows the three components of total return equation in conceptual form and in more precise mathematical form. The term "g" is the growth rate (percent per year) for earnings per share, the change in the PE ratio is shown as "ΔPE" as a percent per year change and the dividend yield (shown as a percent) is the third term.

This three part equation for projecting your total return over any time horizon is quite simple yet profound. It forces you to individually focus on each of the three components of your return in lieu of just vaguely expecting some return to magically materialize. The PE is a specialty term that needs tender loving care in its determination. I believe that the perception of inflation, the expected earnings growth rate and the consistency of the earnings growth are key to a proper determination of the PE change. PE is not an arbitrary fallout of where earnings and/or price happen to go. PE is very deliberately determined in the huge voting booth called the stock market. That is, PE is the valuation placed on the earnings. In this regard, we usually think of earnings per share as opposed to total corporate earnings.

Chart 2 depicts the Coca-Cola stock over the 35 years 1968 into 2003 inclusive. This period is shown because it dramatically shows an interesting earnings, price and PE history. The earnings per share scale (left vertical axis) and the stock price scale (right vertical axis) are set up so that any time the stock price touches the earnings line, the PE at that time is 15. A logarithmic vertical scale is used so that a straight line trend is a constant rate of growth. You can easily visualize when the PE moves above 15 (price above earnings) and when it moves below 15 (price below earnings).

The PE was high and in a general expansion over the 1968 through 1972 period, a general decline over 1973 through 1981 and an expansion again over the period 1982 into 1998. The small table in the upper left corner of Chart 2 gives the compound average annual price change for each of four time periods along with the two components of price change: earnings per share (EPS) change and PE change. The two terms, earnings average annual percent change and PE average annual percent change are multiplicative to get price change. That is, over 1973 through 1981 the price change is:

$(1 + (9.5/100)) \times (1 + (-16.4/100)) = .915$

which equates to an average annual price decline of -8.5%. The equation could have been written to arrive directly at this result by a using a couple more terms.

The point is to see how the price change was broken into the two components of earnings change and PE change. Of course, the overall assumption is that a stock price tends to go where earnings go except for valuation (PE) changes. These two components work together to make the price change. Of course, the total return is percent price change plus percent dividend yield.

All of this works for any stock over any time period. The focus is then on forecasting earnings growth, PE change and dividend yield. The mystery term to many people is the PE change. This series of chapters will shine definitive light on how to approach the task of attempting to forecast PE changes in a future trend sense.

Chart 1

Conceptually,

R = EPS Growth Rate (%) + Divd. Yield (%) +/- Δ PE (%)

Mathematically,

$$R = ((((1 + g/100) \times (1 + \Delta PE/100)) - 1) \times 100) + \text{Divd. Yield}$$

Over approximately 30 years, the PE term falls out.

Eads and Heald Investment Counsel

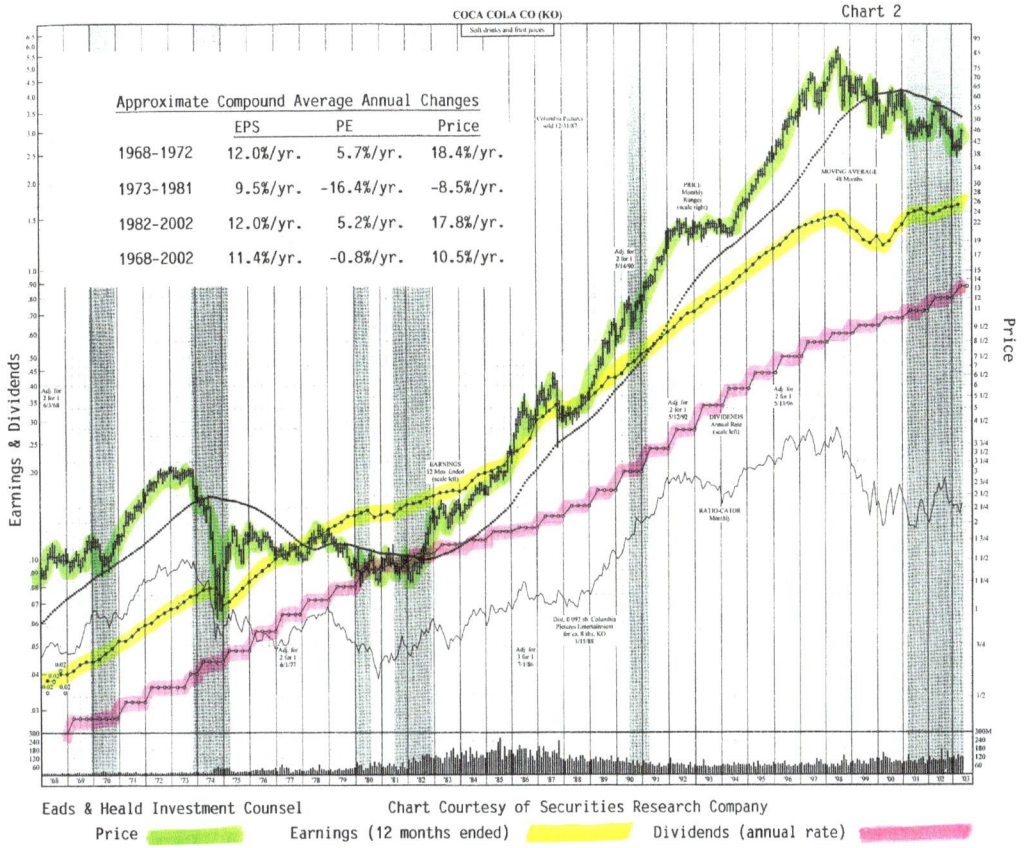

COCA COLA CO (KO)

Chart 2

Approximate Compound Average Annual Changes

	EPS	PE	Price
1968-1972	12.0%/yr.	5.7%/yr.	18.4%/yr.
1973-1981	9.5%/yr.	-16.4%/yr.	-8.5%/yr.
1982-2002	12.0%/yr.	5.2%/yr.	17.8%/yr.
1968-2002	11.4%/yr.	-0.8%/yr.	10.5%/yr.

Eads & Heald Investment Counsel   Chart Courtesy of Securities Research Company

Price   Earnings (12 months ended)   Dividends (annual rate)

Chapter 7: Short-Term vs. Long-Term Investing

Simply stated, common stocks are not suited for a short-term approach. I would compare short-term investing to a fool's game. Using inside information is illegal and one is competing against other bright, well informed and greedy people. They could possibly be brighter, better informed and greedier than you.

There are a large number of professional investors vying to manage large investment funds and they are all attempting to perform well over a period as short as two to three to five years in order to keep the funds they have and to gain new funds. This is in spite of the fact that a given investment style might well be out of favor for a time period much longer than five years. The point is that you have stiff competition. However, you have one excellent advantage as an individual. You do not get fired from overseeing your own funds if you do not perform well over, say, three years. Thus, you have the possible luxury (depending on your age) to invest looking out five to ten to twenty years or more. More times than not, this is not the focus of the big outfits. Many of them work under a "perform or die" rule.

So, how does a long-term approach help you? In this series of chapters it will be shown that there are long-term trends at work and certain factors appear to be directly dependent on other factors. These insights will be based on empirical history and not on some arcane "wave theory" or such. Our work comes under the heading that history has a lot to teach us if we will observe and learn. Further than just blindly using historical relationships we want to be able to explain why the relationships make sense.

Unfortunately, much of the year-by-year data relevant to equity investing is full of "noise". That is, while there may well be an underlying trend at work in a data series the year-by-year data may mask the trend by bouncing around and fooling both the eye and the brain. As you will later see, we overcome this "noise" factor by using moving averages of data. Out of apparent chaos can appear a logical trend. This gets back to our endorsement of longer-term trend investing.

There is another very real bonus to longer-term investing. The amount of portfolio trading (turnover) tends to go way down. This saves the investor money on trading costs. Also, much of the research time spent on examining short-term jiggles in stock fundamentals can more productively be spent on studying long-term trend fundamentals.

Chapter 8: Semi-log versus Linear Graph Paper

Quite possibly, you know about semi-log (i.e., logarithmic) graph paper. However, if you are not familiar with it, we should discuss it briefly since semi-log graphs are used frequently in economic, investment and finance literature.

Semi-log means just that.....a partially logarithmic scale. Typically, the horizontal "x" axis is a linear scale with equal spacing for equal units. However, the vertical "y" axis is not a linear scaling…it is a logarithmic scale. For instance, the vertical scale of a chart would be 1, 10, 100, 1000 etc. with each of these the same distance apart. The log (to base 10) of each of these is, respectively, 0, 1, 2, 3, etc. In many situations the vertical log scale gives an intuitively more natural impression of the data at hand than using a vertical linear scale.

Simply stated, the logarithmic scale allows a constant rate of growth to appear as a straight line. With a linear (non logarithmic) vertical scale a positive constant rate of growth line will bend upward over time.

See Chart 1 (semi-log) and Chart 2 (linear) where each chart plots a line beginning at 75 in the first time period and growing at a rate of 30% per year. The value reaches 1,344 in the twelfth time period. In the linear vertical scale Chart 2 the data line bends upward while in the log scale Chart 1 the 30% growth line is straight. It is often useful to be able to view a constant rate of growth as a straight line. One good example would the annual earnings growth rate for a corporation. If the earnings growth rate is constant at, say, 30% percent per year, a line bending upward would give a misleading impression of growing faster and faster. A straight line would give the correct impression of steady growth at a constant rate.

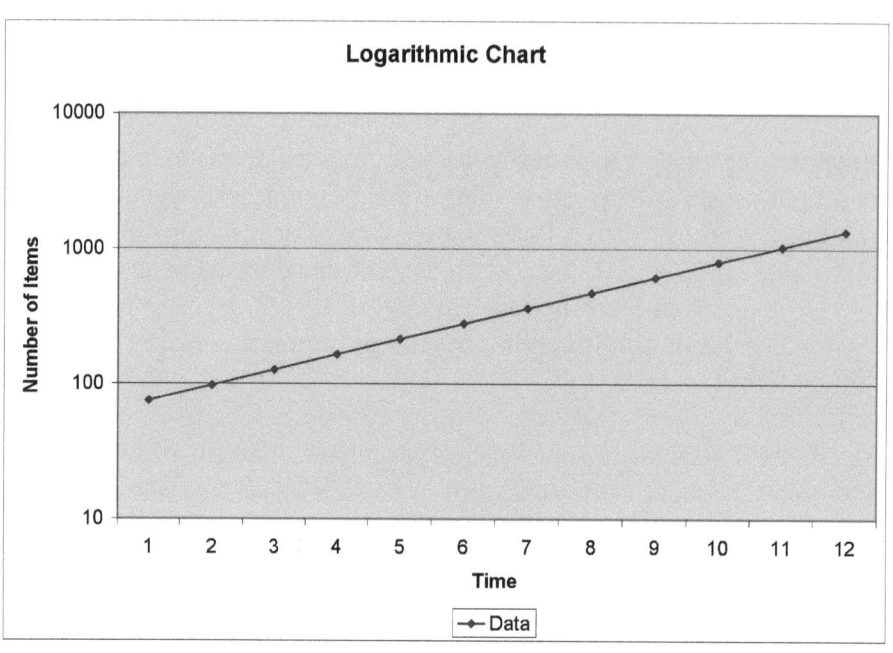

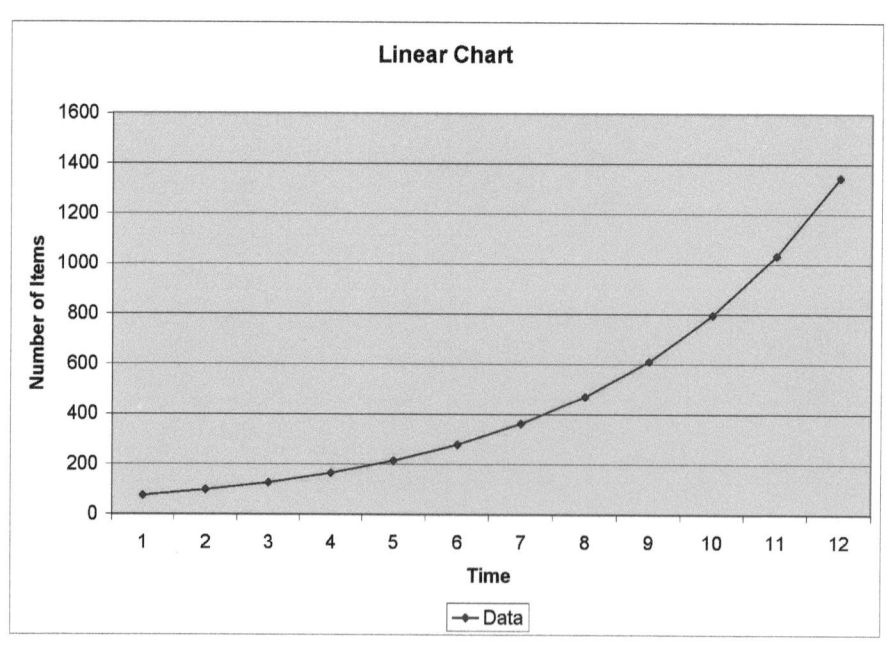

Chapter 9: Growth in Wealth: Stocks, Bonds, T-Bills and Inflation

It is useful to be aware of how key financial assets have appreciated and built wealth over the years. This can instill confidence for difficult times as well as assist you in constructing a portfolio that is appropriate for a particular stage of your life.

Herein, stocks are the Standard & Poor's 500 index of stocks (Cowles Commission Stocks prior to 1926), bonds are high quality corporate bonds with 20 years to maturity and treasury bills are simply 90 day Treasury bills. The comparative inflation is the U.S. Consumer Price Index.

We use a semi-log graph so we can easily spot any constant rates of growth in wealth accumulation. Stock and bond returns are total returns. That is, stock returns include price appreciation along with dividend yield. Bonds include price changes as well as interest paid. Treasury bills are issued at a discount off of par and the appreciation to par over 90 days is the rate of return.

Examine Chart 1. All four entities are started at the end of year 1900 with one unit of value. Think of it as $1. The original $1 in stocks becomes $19,097.2 over the 110 years. This is a return of 9.4% per year. For bonds, the $1 becomes $426.4 for a return of 5.7% per year. Another way to view the numbers is to think of starting with $10,000 at the end of 1900 becoming $191.0 million for stocks or $4.3 million for bonds where taxes are ignored in both cases. This is a big difference! Of course, 110 years is a long life of exercising, no smoking and eating right.

The 90 day treasury bills go from $1 to $61.5 for a 3.8% per year return. $10,000 would grow to $615,000 over the 110 years. Risk and return go hand in hand. The investment with the greatest risk, or volatility, makes the most money over the long haul. However, the higher returns result in more uncertainty and anguish along the way. Plus, inflation moves along over the 110 years at a rate of 3.1% per year. This removes a lot of the purchasing power of the various returns. The real return (above inflation) for stocks is 6.3% per year, for bonds it is 2.6% per year and for T-bills it is only 0.7% per year return above the ravages of inflation. Inflation cannot be ignored in any plan to accumulate wealth and purchasing power.

Look at Chart 2. This shows the year-by-year returns for each of the three investment vehicles from Chart 1. Far and away, stocks have the most upside/downside volatility (sleepless nights) over the years.   The treasury bills have the lowest year-by-year volatility.

Notice in Chart 1 how bond returns (wealth accumulation) begin to pick up around the year 1980. Now, notice in Chart 2 how the annual up/down volatility of bond returns also starts to increase in 1980.

Accept the axiom that risk (volatility) of returns goes hand-in-hand with higher long-term returns. There is no free and easy lunch. But, this makes sense. How could it work in any other way? Stocks are not a crapshoot or rigged casino. Stocks behave in a very orderly fashion. Stocks are disparaged by silly people who misuse stocks to attempt to make short-term gains without understanding the nature of the beast. In fact, over time, stocks are an "upward meandering beast". Ultimately, stock prices go where earnings go. Add in the return from dividends paid out and allow enough time for changes in price to earnings ratio to wash out so the result is Return = Earnings Growth + Dividend Yield (refer back to Chapter 6).

Chart 1

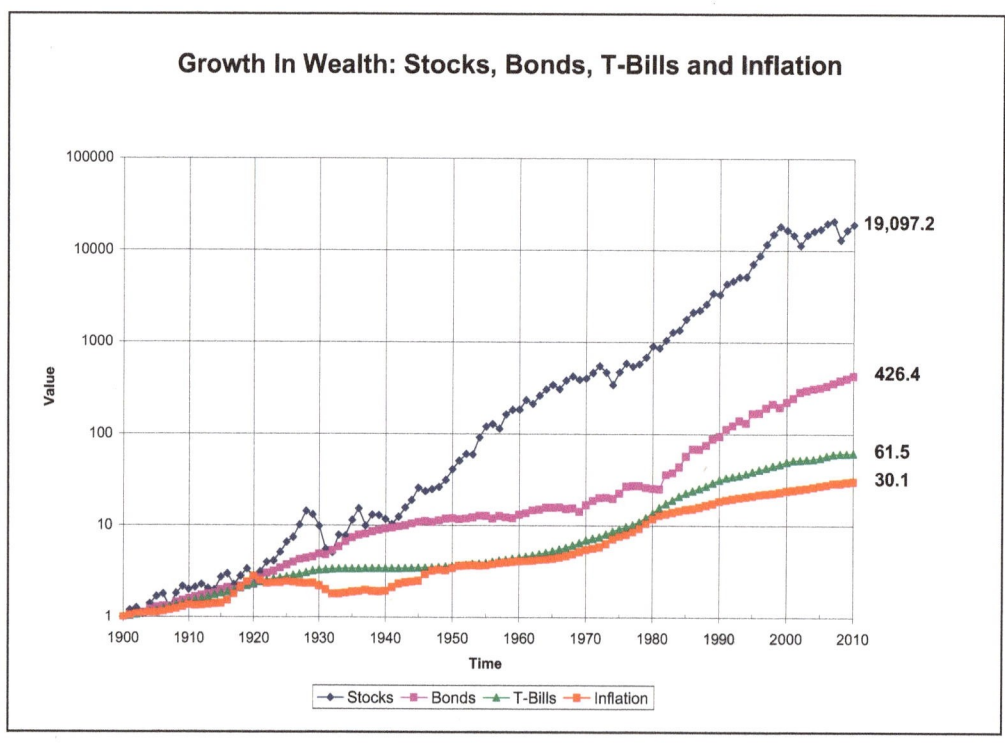

Chart 2

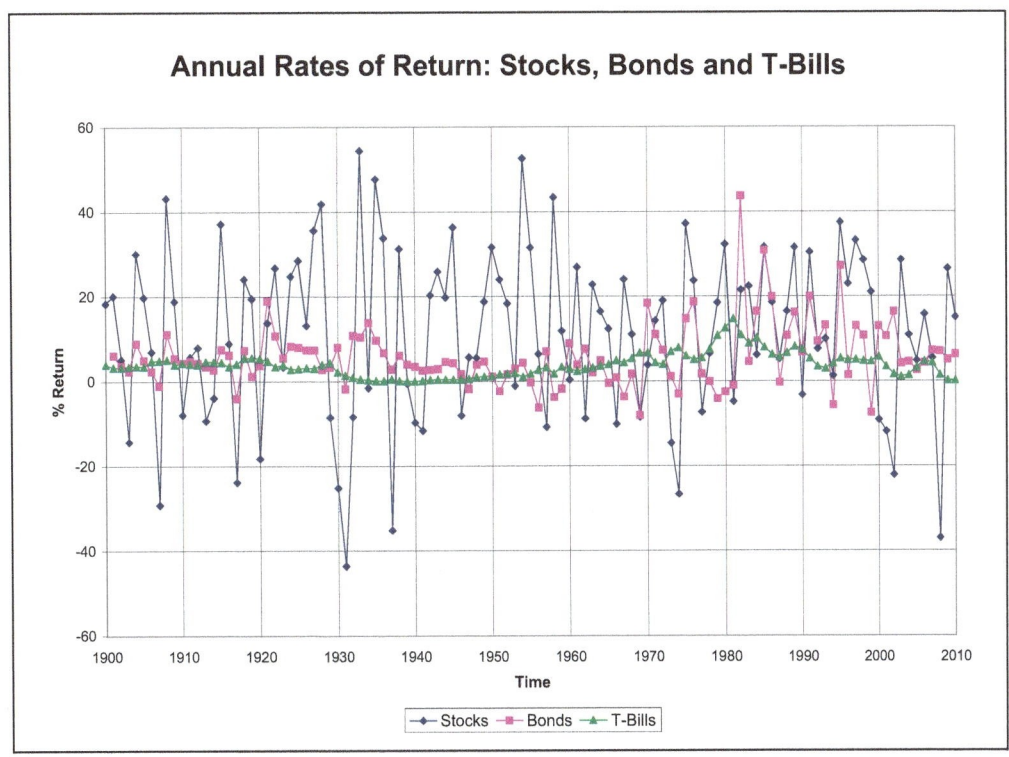

Chapter 10: Inflation and Interest Rates vs. PE

We need to define the term price/earnings (PE) ratio. This factor is key to understanding the workings of stocks. To simplify, a company has net earnings. Divided by the number of shares of stock outstanding we have earnings per share. A price/earnings ratio is the multiplier times current earnings per share to arrive at the current stock price per share. It is a valuation placed on current earnings. A PE ratio is not simply a fallout of whatever happens to be the current price per share divided by the current earnings per share. The PE is deliberately determined by the mass of all investors. It should be noted that some investors cast their vote on a fair PE for a stock better informed than other investors when they purchase a stock. The fallout factor is the stock price. The price results from multiplying the PE times earnings per share. Later, I will go into some detail as to how I believe investors determine a fair PE for a stock. First, we need to consider some other ideas.

Conventional wisdom on Wall Street is that price/earnings ratios (PE's) are dramatically impacted by interest rates. To that belief I put forth Chart 1. Everything shown in this chart is for running 10 year time periods so as to smooth out year-to-year noise and allow us to focus on trends. The top chart panel shows both long-term interest rates (high grade 20 year corporate bonds) and short-term interest rates (90 day Treasury Bills). The middle panel shows consumer price inflation and the bottom panel shows the PE for the Standard & Poor's 500 index (Cowles Commission Stocks prior to 1926).

First, let us examine the belief that PE's are largely determined by interest rates. A relationship is difficult to discern. Focus on the 30 year period 1950-1980. Both long and short interest rates steadily trended upward while PE's made a complete roundtrip from low to high and back to low. Some years ago on viewing these charts, the world renowned partners/strategists at a top Wall Street investment firm said to me that no one cares about these long-term trends. They stated that they have a difficult time looking out 6-12 months in their forecasting and that their clients were only looking out 1-2 years. Certainly, maintaining a shorter focus and avoiding longer trends is an advantage to a securities trading desk.

Regardless of your time range of interest you are riding on the PE trend curve. Over any given single year you may be trending up, trending down, topping or bottoming. Given the running 10 year trend picture of PE that spans 140 years of data, only a very silly, ignorant or dishonest person would not have some interest in the determinants of this PE picture.

Throughout all of my work, two beliefs are very important. First, investors are always fighting the last battle. That is, they have a difficult time believing that a trend has altered direction. It seems to take 5-7 years for them to accept that a trend direction has changed. Second, it is the "perception" of something that rules and not necessarily what is actually happening at the time. An example of these two concepts would be the fact that inflation in the U.S. actually began relentlessly rising in the mid-1960's boosted by the spending on the Great Society, the Vietnam War and the Man on the Moon project. However, it took seven years and the oil embargo before investors accepted that inflation was truly a problem and they began adjusting stock PE's to this fact.

Now, look at the relationship between inflation and PE. A dramatic visual relationship exists. Of course, this is not scientific assurance that the trend in inflation helps to determine the trend in PE. However, the fact is that peaks in trend inflation are followed a few years later by a bottom in PE and, conversely, a bottom in inflation is followed a few years later by a peak in PE. The relationship is dramatic enough to attempt to construct a cause/effect model.

The belief that PE's are inversely related to interest rates is essentially based on the idea that higher interest rates pull money out of stocks and into fixed income investments. In the sense that a current stock price is the present value of future earnings, the discount rate (the rate used to bring future earnings back to present value) is directly tied to current interest rates. Thus, when interest rates go up, the present value of future earnings goes down. Conversely, when interest rates go down, the present value of future earnings goes up. In other words, PE is up when interest rates are low and PE is down when interest rates are high. Unfortunately, long-term history offers no support to this thesis.

How could it be that regardless of interest rates the trend in stock PE's seem to key off of inflation? Inflation makes a dollar in the future worth less than it would be worth with no inflation. When investors view a current stock price as the present value of a future stream of earnings, possibly they view inflation as the key factor in bringing future dollars back to a present value regardless of interest rates.

Granted, intuition might cause one to believe that when the lure of higher interest rates pulls money out of stocks, PE's should fall. However, it just may be that investors take their initial cue from inflation. That is, higher inflation leads investors to "expect" higher interest rates and lower inflation leads investors to "expect" lower interest rates. Whether or not interest rates actually follow inflation up and down may be academic if the "expectation" of a relationship exists and investors act on that belief. Or, it may just be that the discount rate used to discount a future stream of earnings and/or dividends back to present value is the rate of inflation as opposed to a key interest rate figure.

Let us pursue the belief that it is the perception of future inflation that serves as the discount rate in bringing future earnings back to present value in search of a fair PE. The question arises as to how far out into the future investors are willing to discount future earnings back to present value to determine a PE. Common sense would dictate that when investors are feeling generally optimistic they will be willing to look out further. Conversely, when they are troubled, they will look out a shorter time period. Of course, many factors can go into determining optimism or pessimism. My simple model here assumes that only the perception of future trend inflation determines how far out one discounts future earnings back to present value. That is, when inflation is assumed to be high (say, 10% like in the late 1970's) investors only discount out approximately 8 years. When inflation is assumed to be low (say, 1% like in the 1960's) investors discount out approximately 16 years.

Charts 2, 3 and 4 display some simplistic determinations of PE in three different inflation environments. Chart 2 follows $1.00 in current earnings per share growing at 15% per year and having each future year's earnings brought back to present value using the assumed rate of inflation of 1% per year. Summing up 16 years of such earnings gives a present value of future earnings of $57.34. If this is a fair current stock price then having started with $1.00 of current earnings per share the fair PE is $57.34/$1.00 or a PE of 57.34. Divided by the 15% growth rate, it is considered that a fair PE is 3.82 times the earnings growth rate. In fact, this is where quality growth stocks (i.e., Nifty Fifty) went to by the early 1970's. Chart 4 shows the other extreme. Inflation is assumed at 10% per year and future earnings are only considered out through 8 years. The current fair PE is calculated to be 9.82 or .65 times the 15% growth rate. This is where quality growth stock PE's trended to by the late 1970's.

Chart 3 better represents where we may typically be in the process of determining a fair PE. With 3% inflation, 12 years are used and the fair PE is 1.76 times the growth rate. I would use a range of 1.5 to 2.0 times the growth rate.

Of course, the above model is very simplistic. No mention is made of the consistency of the earnings growth. That is, two companies could both have a 15% trend earnings growth rate. However, one could have a straight line trend growth while the other company could see its earnings bounce up and down year-to-year while still maintaining a 15% trend. Obviously, the more consistent grower should be accorded a higher PE all other things being equal.

Even with their simplicity, the views expressed above regarding the relationship of inflation and PE are quite profound and should prompt much more research in this direction if not immediately changing the focus from believing that interest rates determine PE's to one believing that the perception of future trend inflation is the key factor in the long-term trend of PE's.

Chart 5 plots PE vs. inflation for four different growth rates. Note that for higher growth rates, the fair PE falls faster as inflation increases than is the case for lower growth rates. Conversely, as inflation falls, PE's increase more rapidly for faster growing companies. This chart helps to conceptually visualize what happened to the PE's of the Nifty Fifty growth stocks in the early 1970's as the perception of inflation went from nonexistent inflation to 3%, 4%, 5% and upward. However, the results in this chart have been altered somewhat from the type of equations indicated in Charts 2, 3 and 4. This was done to combine the equations theoretical results with empirical historical results. One could argue that the Nifty Fifty stocks were not overpriced in selling at PE's of 3-4 times their growth rates so long as inflation was perceived as nonexistent. However, as the perception of inflation markedly increased, PE's began a long slide.

Since one is not likely to be successful in predicting year-to-year PE ratios, it would seem that the more useful exercise would be to determine if one is in a long-term trend PE expansion or a long-term trend PE contraction. In long periods of PE expansion, growth stock PE's have great upside leverage while in long periods of PE contraction, they have great downside leverage. Although outside the scope of this chapter, this leverage effect can be easily demonstrated by discounting a stream of high growth rate earnings back to present value using a high discount rate versus a low discount rate. Start with unitized earnings of $1 per share so that the resulting sum of all future earnings brought back to present value (i.e., price) divided by the current $1 per share earnings is the PE ratio. The next time you run across a guru level strategist that says that PE's are controlled by interest rates, ask him to explain why history does not bear this out. Tell him that you are not so much interested in his theory of "what should be," but are much more interested in a thesis that jives with a long period of real life history. Don't let him off the hook until you get a satisfactory answer. Wall Street has an amazing blind spot on this matter. It is as if it would be heresy to not believe that PE's are controlled by interest rates. Believing that the long-term trend in interest rates controls the long-term trend in PE's is very much akin to believing that the world is flat and you will fall over the edge if you attempt to sail around the world. If everyone believes something, you appear a fool if you express a contrary view. In this instance, we have high resolution satellite photo reconnaissance of the world and we know that there is not a good correlation between interest rates and PE's.

As discussed elsewhere, a successful Wall Street strategist is one who garners big commissions for his firm. Weight is given to many factors in addition to being a seemingly adequate forecaster. Viewers are not attracted to certain TV weathermen because of accurate forecasts but because they are colorful, entertaining and are adept in engaging in mindless verbal prattle with the anchorperson. After all, a Wall Street strategist is in "show business." Image, not substance, is the key. Some will disparage long-term trend analysis by saying that investors are concerned about what will happen over the next year or two, not over the next decade. This is a akin to being a rowboat on the middle of the ocean and saying that you do not care which way the tidal current is taking you. That is, you only care about the waves slapping against the sides of your boat. True, large waves can sink you and you must be mindful of them. But, to ignore the tidal drift, you have absolutely no control over your destiny. In other words, if a strong trend direction for PE's is in process and it may span 10-15 years in one direction, how can you ignore the trend and still be a knowledgeable investor? If the trend is 10-15 years in duration you would do well to clue in to what is happening.

Chart 1

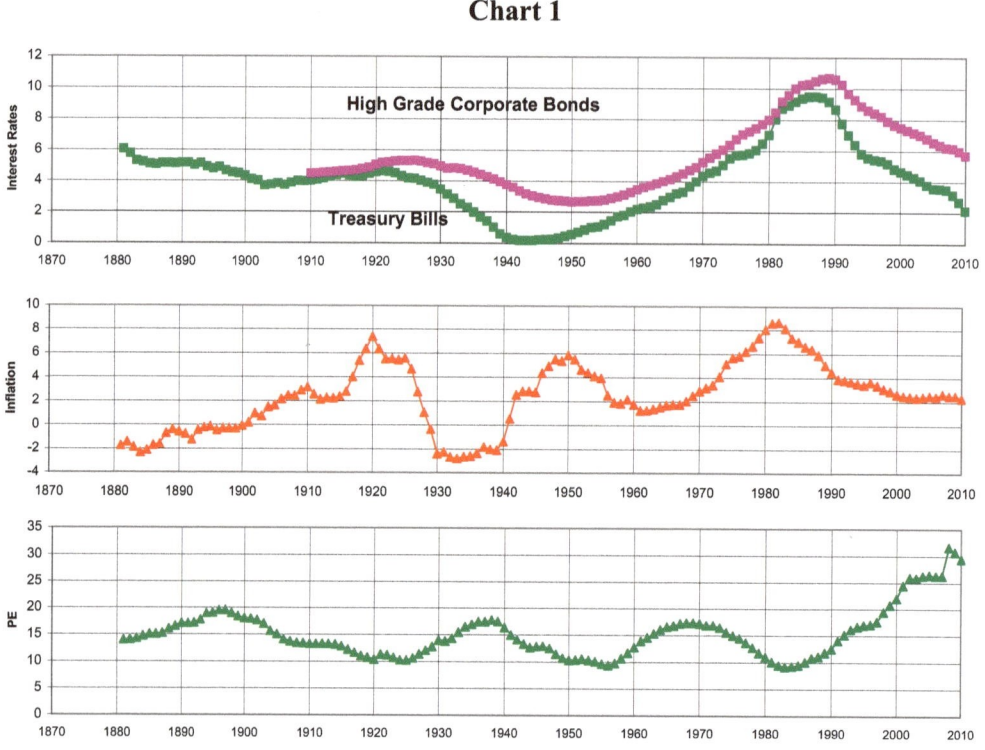

Chart 2

INFLATION	1	%
GROWTH	15	%

Year	EPS Growth 15%	PV
0	1.00	1.00
1	1.15	1.14
2	1.32	1.30
3	1.52	1.48
4	1.75	1.68
5	2.01	1.91
6	2.31	2.18
7	2.66	2.48
8	3.06	2.82
9	3.52	3.22
10	4.05	3.66
11	4.65	4.17
12	5.35	4.75
13	6.15	5.41
14	7.08	6.16
15	8.14	7.01
16	9.36	7.98
17	10.76	9.09
18	12.38	10.35
19	14.23	11.78
20	16.37	13.41

	PE	PE/g
5 Yrs.	7.51	0.50
6 Yrs.	9.68	0.65
7 Yrs.	12.17	0.81
8 Yrs.	14.99	1.00
9 Yrs.	18.21	1.21
10 Yrs.	21.87	1.46
11 Yrs.	26.04	1.74
12 Yrs.	30.79	2.05
13 Yrs.	36.19	2.41
14 Yrs.	42.35	2.82
15 Yrs.	49.36	3.29
16 Yrs.	57.34	3.82
17 Yrs.	66.43	4.43
18 Yrs.	76.77	5.12
19 Yrs.	88.55	5.90
20 Yrs.	101.96	6.80

Chart 3

INFLATION	3	%
GROWTH	15	%

Year	EPS Growth 15%	PV
0	1.00	1.00
1	1.15	1.12
2	1.32	1.25
3	1.52	1.39
4	1.75	1.55
5	2.01	1.74
6	2.31	1.94
7	2.66	2.16
8	3.06	2.41
9	3.52	2.70
10	4.05	3.01
11	4.65	3.36
12	5.35	3.75
13	6.15	4.19
14	7.08	4.68
15	8.14	5.22
16	9.36	5.83
17	10.76	6.51
18	12.38	7.27
19	14.23	8.12
20	16.37	9.06

	PE	PE/g
5 Yrs.	7.04	0.47
6 Yrs.	8.98	0.60
7 Yrs.	11.14	0.74
8 Yrs.	13.56	0.90
9 Yrs.	16.25	1.08
10 Yrs.	19.27	1.28
11 Yrs.	22.63	1.51
12 Yrs.	26.38	1.76
13 Yrs.	30.57	2.04
14 Yrs.	35.25	2.35
15 Yrs.	40.47	2.70
16 Yrs.	46.30	3.09
17 Yrs.	52.81	3.52
18 Yrs.	60.08	4.01
19 Yrs.	68.20	4.55
20 Yrs.	77.26	5.15

Chart 4

INFLATION	10	%
GROWTH	15	%

Year	EPS Growth 15%	PV
0	1.00	1.00
1	1.15	1.05
2	1.32	1.09
3	1.52	1.14
4	1.75	1.19
5	2.01	1.25
6	2.31	1.31
7	2.66	1.37
8	3.06	1.43
9	3.52	1.49
10	4.05	1.56
11	4.65	1.63
12	5.35	1.70
13	6.15	1.78
14	7.08	1.86
15	8.14	1.95
16	9.36	2.04
17	10.76	2.13
18	12.38	2.23
19	14.23	2.33
20	16.37	2.43

	PE	PE/g
5 Yrs.	5.72	0.38
6 Yrs.	7.03	0.47
7 Yrs.	8.40	0.56
8 Yrs.	9.82	0.65
9 Yrs.	11.31	0.75
10 Yrs.	12.87	0.86
11 Yrs.	14.50	0.97
12 Yrs.	16.21	1.08
13 Yrs.	17.99	1.20
14 Yrs.	19.85	1.32
15 Yrs.	21.80	1.45
16 Yrs.	23.84	1.59
17 Yrs.	25.97	1.73
18 Yrs.	28.19	1.88
19 Yrs.	30.52	2.03
20 Yrs.	32.95	2.20

Chart 5

PE vs. Inflation

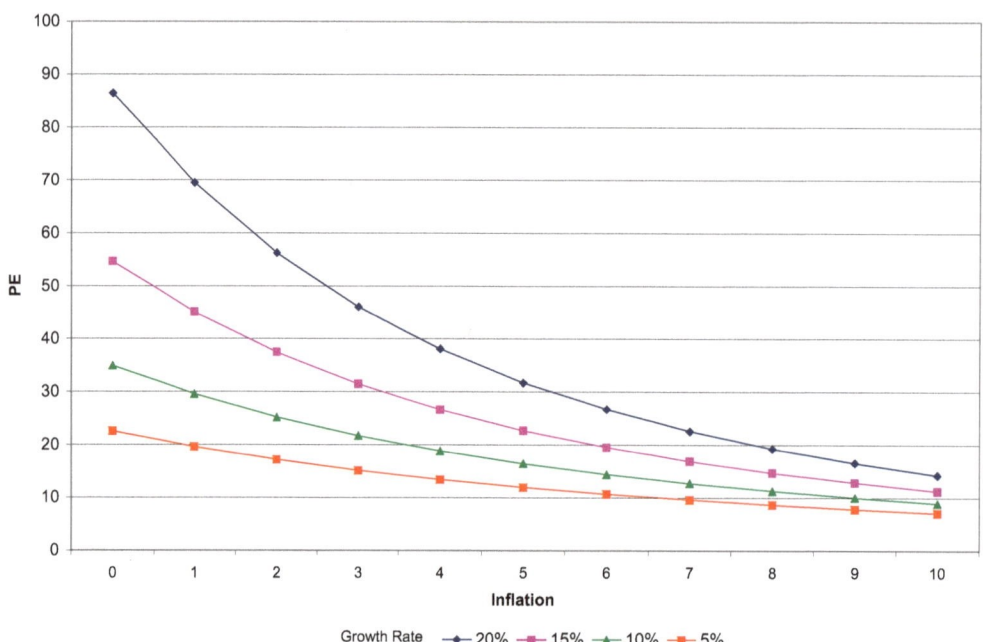

Chapter 11: Stock Prices Ultimately Go Where Earnings Go

Ultimately, stock prices go where earnings go. Chart 1 shows the trend in Standard & Poor's 500 price and earnings (Cowles Commission Stocks prior to 1926). Inflation is also shown. Running 10 year averages are used and the values are all indexed to 1.0 at the start. The running 10 year averages allow us to focus on the underlying trends and not have our focus diverted by short-term noise in the data.

Note that after over 100 years stock prices continue to track along with earnings. Both prices and earnings gradually pull away from inflation. You see that as inflation inflects upward, the price tends to move up slower than earnings. This is a period of PE contraction per Chart 1 in Chapter 10. When inflation slows down, the price tends to move up faster than earnings. This is a period of PE expansion per Chart 1 in Chapter 10. Nonetheless, over this very long time period displayed price and earnings keep coming back together and price ultimately goes where earnings go.

Chart 2 shows a year-to-year picture of earnings progression and inflation since World War II. A trend relationship between earnings and inflation can be discerned as with the prior 10 year moving average chart. As inflation increases from the mid 1960's through the 1970's, the trend in earnings growth also increases. As inflation slows down beginning in the early 1980's, the earnings trend also slows down. Still, Chart 1 using 10 year moving averages makes it much easier to view trends as the short-term noise is smoothed out.

The message here is simply that over the long-term stock prices will go where earnings go. However, over the short and intermediate term inflation will cause price-to-earnings (PE) ratios to trend up and trend down. Thus, earnings and price gradually move above and below each other over time. Increasing inflation tends to result in declining PE's while declining inflation typically sees a period of rising PE's. The key is for long-term investors to own a very diversified (35 or more) stocks and monitor them to weed out those with decaying trend fundamentals. Shorter term market, or individual stock, timing/trading never makes sense.

Over time periods of 15 or so years there may well be an opportunity to be in the type stocks that will most benefit from either a declining or rising trend in inflation. In short, growth stocks typically benefit from long periods of declining inflation and rising PE's. More on this later.

Chart 1

Wealth Indices - 10 Year Moving Average

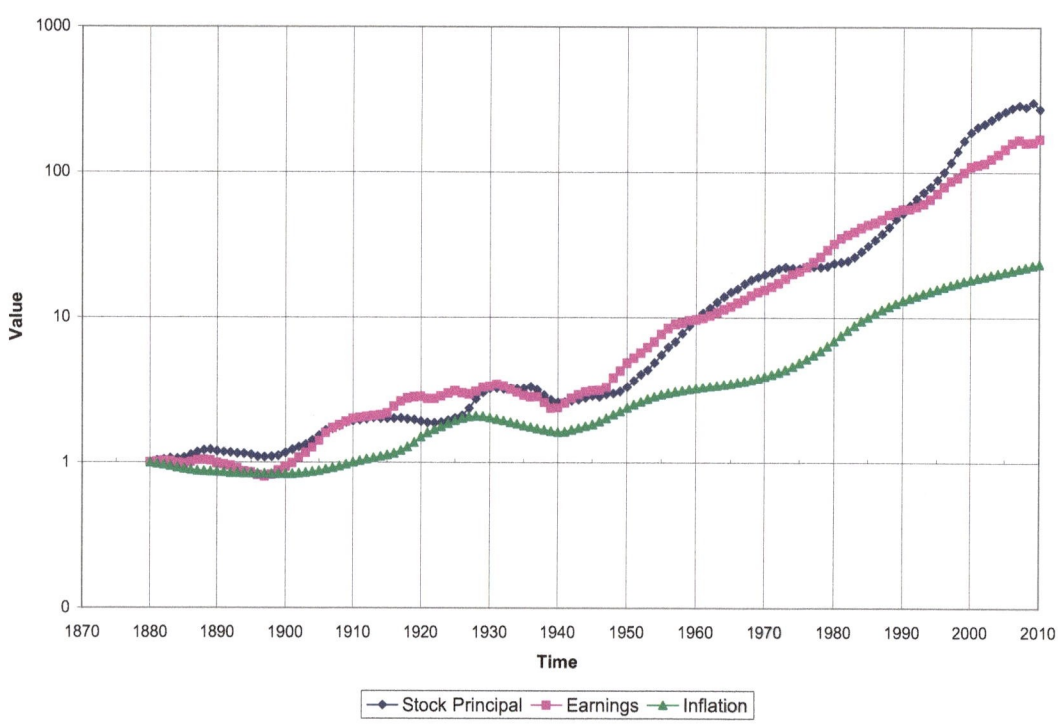

Chart 2

S&P 500 E.P.S. and CPI Cumulative Index

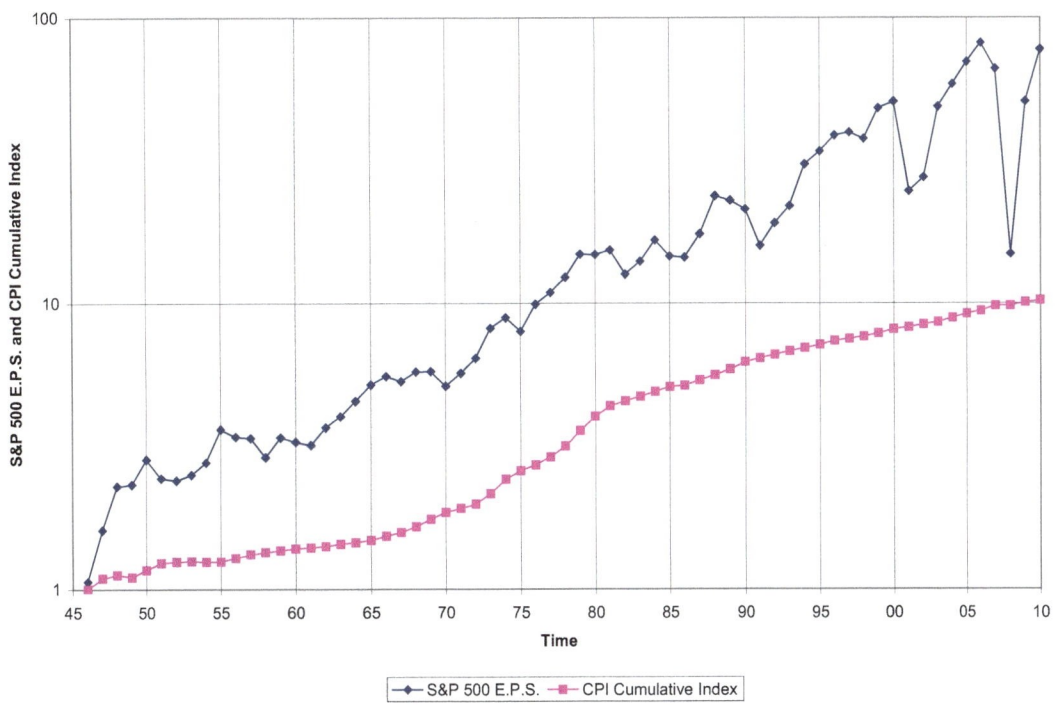

Chapter 12: Inflation Momentum and Stock Market Returns

We have developed a simple methodology for looking at the trend in Consumer Price Inflation free from the year-to-year ups and downs. The focus is on determining when the long-term trend in inflation has reached a major top or a major bottom. Ideally, there should be no false indicators along the way. The top portion of Chart 1 displays what can be called Inflation Momentum.

It is useful and interesting to concurrently look at the total return (price change and dividends) on the Standard & Poor's 500 stock index for running 10 year periods. The bottom portion of Chart 1 displays this. Note that this chart shows the return for the following 10 years. For example, the point at 2000 is the total average annual return from the end of 2000 through 2010.

The long-term average annual total return on the S&P 500 has been approximately 10% per year. However, note in Chart 1 that very little time is actually spent at this 10% average. Returns range from down near 0% up to 20% over 10 year time periods.

In comparing inflation momentum to stock returns in Chart 1, it is readily seen that a major top in inflation is followed by good long-term S&P 500 returns while a major bottom in inflation is followed by poor long-term returns. This makes intuitive sense if you accept inflation as the primary discount mechanism in bringing future earnings back to present value. While rising inflation boosts earnings growth to varying degrees (depending on the industry), it also squashes price/earnings (PE) multiples. This is a result of future earnings having lower present value in a period of higher inflation. The net result is negative for stock prices.

There has been a major bottom in Inflation Momentum within the past few years. This is because our political/economic system is such that it makes it difficult to be vigilant over what was seen as a non-problem -- inflation. The Federal Reserve Board is currently more concerned about promoting economic growth than with staving off future inflation. The current low valuation for the U.S. dollar will tend to increase inflationary pressures via imports. Also, the fact that inflation has been so low for so long make that a tough act to follow. In other words, a continuation of very low inflation will be difficult to perpetuate. Since inflation momentum has bottomed, it is very likely that the following 10 years will generally be very frustrating for equity investors (certainly for owners of S&P 500 index funds). Value stocks will respond somewhat differently than growth stocks to the changes. It will be very important to have a solid understanding of how these two distinct equity investment styles (growth and value) respond to changes in the trend of inflation. Also, the time lags involved are very important as to how they affect growth stocks versus value stocks.

Chart 1

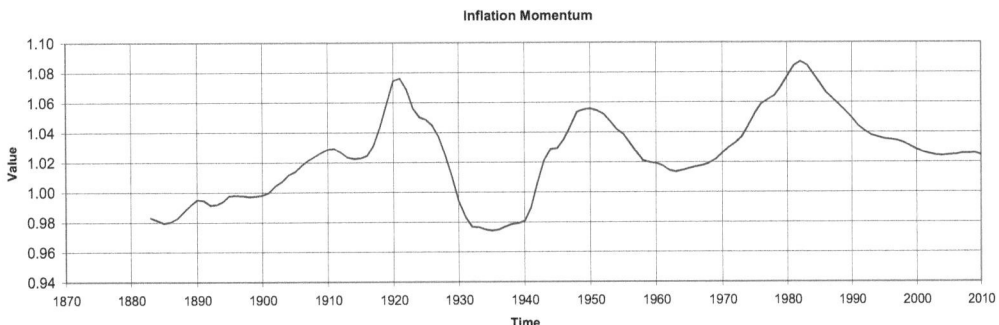

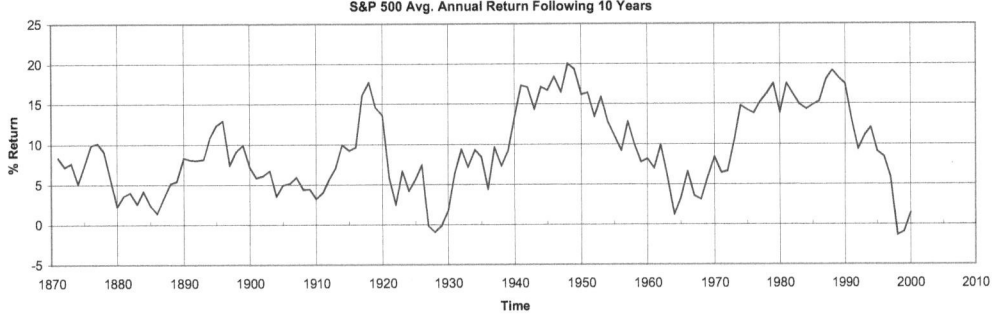

Chapter 13: A Computer Generated Fair Value Channel

Back in the early 1980's while at the Wellington Management Company, I put forth my first Fair Value Channel. It was a channel with a dramatic rise through the 1980's and on into the 1990's as I expected inflation to peak soon and for a major PE expansion to take place. The staff at Wellington heard my views on this ad nauseam. I was forecasting the S&P 500 to return 18-20% per year on average in the 1980's and reach a level of 520 by the end of 1994. The S&P 500 generally met these expectations for rate of return in the 1980's and 1990's. My predictions were more on track than most of the seers on Wall Street. The Fair value Channel is not a road to riches. However, it does allow one to focus on two key variables in a trend sense.....earnings growth rates and inflation.

I have continued the concept of the Fair Value Channel and eventually turned it into a computer model. Chart 1 is a Fair Value Channel generated by a computer using earnings growth rates and inflation as the only inputs. The channel width is always kept constant. The solid-colored area is the actual high/low of the S&P 500 each year. This computer generation has done an excellent job of capturing the general trend directions of the stock market over a 72 year time period. To forecast the channel direction going forward, one needs to input projections of trend PE and the S&P 500 earnings growth rate. I believe that the trend in PE is directly determined by the trend in inflation. Thus, in the computer model, the direction of the channel is determined by projections for the earnings growth rate (S&P 500) and inflation. This particular model run assumes that earnings growth returns to the trend growth rate of the period 1940 through 2010 by the end of 2010 and then grows at 6.0% per year compound average through 2020. Inflation is projected at 3.0% for 2012 and then 3.0% per year out through 2020. Chart 2 shows an index for S&P 500 earnings per share with the focus being on 1940 through 2020. The years 2011 through 2020 use estimated earnings. Note how earnings for 2011 through 2020 appear to grow at approximately the same rate as 1940 through 2010.

Earnings growth and PE change are combined in a multiplicative process to arrive at the channel's rate of change:

$$(((1 + g/100) * (1 + \Delta PE/100)) - 1) * 100\%$$

where g = Earnings per share growth rate, and ΔPE = Average annual change in PE

The resulting product represents the trend movement in the channel's direction. Internal in the model is a quantitative relationship between PE and inflation so that the direction of the channel is ultimately only driven by the earnings growth rate and inflation.

I believe that short-term micro market timing is essentially impossible. I do believe that trend market forecasting is very achievable if one focuses on predicting the future trend in inflation and earnings growth.

Given that the large pools of investment money are, or should be, very long-term by nature, this work could be truly dramatic. Individual investors should also focus on the longer-term, but the likelihood is that only a very small percent of individual investors will stay on a successful long-term course. Current wish-list spending and/or chasing the latest year's hot investment style will generally derail their quest.

Chart 1

Fair Value Channel

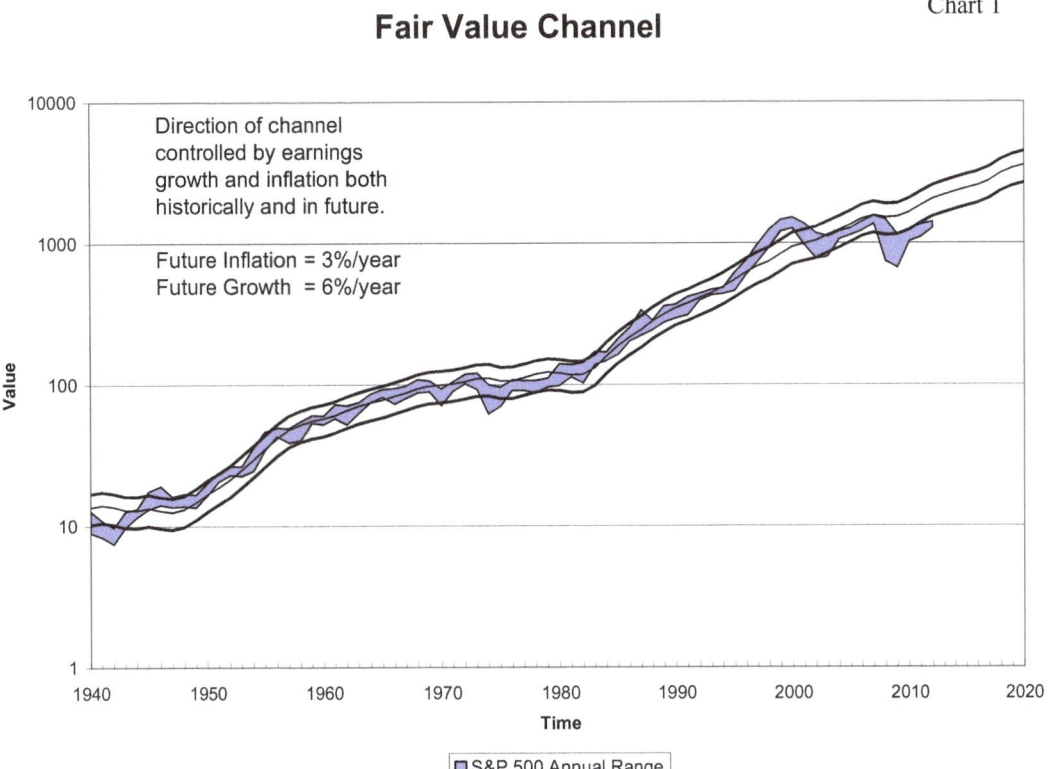

Direction of channel controlled by earnings growth and inflation both historically and in future.

Future Inflation = 3%/year
Future Growth = 6%/year

S&P 500 Annual Range

S&P 500 Earnings Growth Index

Chart 2

Chapter 14: Growth Stocks vs. Value Stocks

When I entered the investment business in 1969, I endorsed the view that one should always adhere to the same equity investment style -- that is, a style with which one is comfortable. On becoming more confident that I understand the factors that bring a style into and out of vogue, I now feel that to adhere to one style for all times is not the most productive approach. The Growth style and the Value style are well defined and different in a major and very fundamental way. History teaches us that when fundamental conditions are right to bring one style into favor, the conditions tend to persist for quite a long time -- say 10-15 years.

You should be very wary of those who attach almost supernatural powers to a portfolio manager primarily because his style is in favor. But, human nature will never change. Investors glorified the prominent growth stock investors in the 1960's and on into the early 1970's far out of proportion to their money management skills once the fact that their style was simply doing great was factored out. Investors did the same thing by glorifying value style investors in the 1970's and into the mid 1980's. In both cases, if the portfolio managers had had their results "style adjusted" (that is, adjust the performance returns caused by the fact that the style was in vogue), they would have appeared more mortal than the immortal powers attributed to them. How bright are they when they proceed to spend the decade following their deification wallowing in sub-par investment results?

One might argue that if your investment time horizon is, say, 30 years, it does not matter which investment style you use. Both will likely lead to a similar result albeit by very different routes along the way. Unfortunately, I have never met any clients so forgiving as to give me 30 years in which to prove myself. So, if your focus is on performing well over 3-5-10 years, you had better have a very definite opinion about which investment style is going to do well and apply that style. Also, beware that style shift junctions can be up to five years in duration. There will not be a neat instantaneous division between the end of one style and the beginning of the new style. It will be a messy and confusing transition filled with doubt. You will need conviction and staying power to adhere to your convictions that a style shift is taking place.

We were in an era where the many investment firms that did so very well from 1972 through 1988 using the value style went into a period of apologizing and predicting that the value style would certainly cycle back into favor "very soon." After all, it was generally not the preferred style for the next 10 years. Some investment firms that use a loose combination of value and growth (that is, the weak form of both) and place tremendous weight on client service can continue to prosper. That is, their investment results are always tolerable as "middle of the road" and they go the extra mile with client service.

Over the years, two major stock investment styles have emerged. The growth stock style focuses on those stocks growing their earnings meaningfully faster than the overall economy and with some degree of consistency. The PE's tend to be higher than the average PE of all stocks and the dividend yields tend to be lower. Debt load tends to be low. The ratio of stock price to book value is generally high. Generally, the companies are in new, vibrant industries and are on the cutting edge of improving the quality of life.

The value stock style uses companies that may be older and somewhat out of favor in the stock market. They tend to pay a dividend yield higher than the norm. A meaningful part of their worth may be in bricks/mortar and real estate. Thus, the ratio of stock price to book value is usually lower than for growth stocks. They tend not to be purchased for their earnings growth rates (unless viewed as a turnaround situation), but for their inherent book value, dividend yield and current low price of the stock. Debt may be a significant part of the total capitalization.

Investors that specialize in buying value stocks may initially screen candidates by looking for those stocks where the projected earnings growth rate plus the dividend yield is greater than two when divided by the PE. For example, a growth rate in earnings of 6% per year coupled with a dividend yield of 6% and a PE of 4 would result in a potentially good value buy. It would deserve some fundamental research to check it out.

Value stock (low PE) investors argue that their style is the best way to invest over the long-term. They say that by concentrating on low PE stocks that usually have a good book value, they seldom take much risk. Also, a significant portion of their total return comes from dividend yield so as to remove a lot of price uncertainty. Certainly, the long-term results for value investing are quite good. However, the long-term results from growth stock investing are also quite good. Which style should you use? Should you simply put half of your funds in each style?

I will argue that if your investment time horizon is 30-35 years, it probably does not matter which style you select. To feel diversified, you could put one half of your funds in each style. For an investor beginning a career-long investment program in his/her 20's or early 30's, a 30-35 year time horizon is not an unreasonable time period. This does not mean that you will not evaluate your results until after 30-35 years have passed. It simply means that the funds will generally not be withdrawn and spent until that period of time has passed.

Chart 1 shows year-by-year total return results from the Vanguard Windsor Fund and the Vanguard U.S. Growth Fund for the 52 years 1959-2010 inclusive. I use Windsor as a proxy for the value style and U.S. Growth as a proxy for the growth style. U.S. Growth fund has had some changes over the years involving international stocks. Here, I only use the domestic results over the entire time period.

The shading on the returns shows which of the two styles had the higher return in each year. The "Index" columns simply accumulate the wealth creation via each style having started with a unit value of 1.000.

You would have been a very smart investor if you had invested solely in growth over the 1959-1972 inclusive period, solely in value over the 1973-1988 inclusive period, growth over 1989-1999 inclusive and value over 2000-2010 inclusive. Your wealth index would have become 1,504.095 for a return of 15.1% per year over the 52 years. Some would argue that having made three style changes over 52 years would have been foolish and unproductive. Certainly, it would never have been completely clear when you should have made a change.

Charts 2, 3, 4 and 5 show the wealth accumulation for the same four sub-periods highlighted in Chart 1. Chart 6 shows the wealth accumulation over the entire 52 years. Chart 7 shows the same results in bar chart form for the four sub-periods and for the entire 52 years.

Let us consider the 30 year period 12/31/58 - 12/31/88 and examine the performance by styles. See Chart 8. The Windsor Fund returned 13.1% per year while the U.S. Growth Fund returned 12.0% per year. Now, let us consider the results if you had switched from growth (U.S. Growth Fund) to value (Windsor Fund) at the end of 1972. Chart 8 shows that your return over the 30 year period would have been 17.0% per year. Obviously, this is a very significant improvement in the 30 year results. Certainly, the chances of having made the switch at exactly the perfect time would have been low. However, what if you had made the change anywhere from three years early to three years late? The chart displays all such results. The average of the seven possible results is 16.2% per year while the worst case is 15.1% per year if you had switched at the end of 1975. In all cases, your 30 year results would have improved markedly over holding either one style for the entire 30 years.

Is it a completely indecipherable mystery what causes the growth stock style to do very well for approximately 15 years and then what causes the value stock style to do very well for approximately 15 years? Is it just random chance and/or irrational investor preferences that cause this to occur? I think not on both counts.

Note in Chart 1 that you would have been even smarter if you had made the style switches so as to capture the best return in each and every year. I would argue that this is an unproductive pursuit and that the short-term style results are somewhat random chance. For example, I would argue that President Clinton came into office in the initial phase of a long growth stock market. However, the economic uncertainty he brought with him coupled with an assault on the health care industry (a paragon of modern growth stock investing) served to lower PE's generally and growth stock PE's in particular over 18-24 months.

I will put forth that the more productive style changes will only occur approximately every 15 or so years. The approximate 30 year cycle seems to appear over and over. The modern U.S. inflation and PE cycles are approximately 30 years. This leads me to suspect a relationship between stock style cycles and inflation/PE cycles.

Review Chapter 10 in regards to a determination of PE's based on inflation and earnings growth rates. In particular, see charts 2 and 4 in Chapter 10. These two charts are both reproduced here as Chart 9. When inflation is at 1% (good times) 16 years of earnings are discounted back to present value. At the other extreme, when inflation is at 10% (bad times), only 8 years of earnings are discounted back to present value. These are assumptions based on associating rising inflation with negative support for PE's and declining inflation with positive support for PE's.

Let's assume that value stocks are generally purchased by more conservative investors who place great value on a meaningful and consistent return from dividend yield. The companies, in turn, appreciate this loyal investor support and want to keep paying a good dividend so long as possible.

On the other hand, assume that growth stocks are typically purchased by investors who seek superior returns through growing the company via reinvesting earnings as opposed to paying a meaningful dividend. So, historically, a meaningful portion of the total return from a "value" stock was from dividend yield. That is, a dividend yield that the companies wanted to avoid cutting if at all possible. Contrarily, a "growth" stock could have almost all of the return from earnings growth and very little, if any, from dividend yield. The result would be that in periods of higher inflation the "value" stock would have a meaningful portion of its total future return (i.e. the dividend yield portion) somewhat insulated from being reduced away.

The essence of my basic model to determine PE's as a function of inflation and earnings growth rates is quite simple. A unitized initial EPS of $1.00 is grown at the earnings growth rate and then each year's EPS is discounted back to present value using the inflation rate. The number of years to sum up (that is, how far out into the future to discount earnings) is a function of inflation. The higher the level of inflation the shorter the discounting. For inflation at 1% I discount out 16 years. For inflation at 10% I discount out 8 years. It is somewhat of a non-linear function of years vs. inflation between 1% and 10% inflation. Since you begin with unitized earnings of $1.00, the sum of the discounted present value (the "price") is the ratio of price/earnings or PE.

Let us use our model governing the PE determination work discussed already that involves inflation, earnings growth rate and discounting future earnings back to present value. We will compare how the PE compresses as inflation goes from 1% to 10% for both a company with 15% earnings growth and one with a 7% earnings growth. In short, generally, when PE's compress they will compress more for faster growing companies and when PE's expand they will expand more for faster growing companies. Using our model:

PE's and PE CHANGES

	Inflation		% Change in PE
	1%	10%	
EPS Growth = 15%	57.3	9.8	-83%
EPS Growth = 7%	27.1	7.1	-74%

Now, let us hypothesize two stocks with each having expected 12% total returns. The value stock has 6% earnings growth and a 6% dividend yield. The growth stock has 10% earnings growth and a 2% dividend yield. The perception of inflation goes from 1% to 10% over 5 years. The value stock PE goes from 24.7 to 6.8 over 5 years which is -23% per year. The growth stock PE goes from 35.7 to 8.0 over five years which is -26% per year. The total average annual return for each stock is:

Value Return = $((((1 + 6/100)*(1 + -23/100)) - 1)*100 + 6)$

$\qquad$ = -12.4% per year over five years

Growth Return = $((((1 + 10/100)*(1 + -26/100)) - 1)*100 + 2)$

$\qquad$ = -16.6% per year over five years

In short, the value style does better in a period of rising trend inflation because the PE is squashed less than for the growth style and less of the total return comes from price change. In a period of falling trend inflation, the growth style would do better. However, bear in mind that investors tend to fight the last battle. Thus, once trend inflation bottoms it may take 5-7 years before the value style takes over. Likewise, once trend inflation tops it may take 5-7 years before the growth style kicks in. Also, a period of rising inflation will tend to favor companies with a lot of real estate and debt on the books as opposed to the contrary. So, value stocks get an added boost in this regard when inflation picks up.

Now, let us use these same two stocks and assume that it takes 15 years for the perception of inflation to go from 1% to 10% and then another 15 years to go back to 1%. Chart 10 shows how the key numbers progress and change over this 30 year time period. Integral to this chart is our model that calculates PE using earnings growth rates and inflation.

Chart 11 plots inflation vs. PE for varying growth rates. The curves in this chart have proprietary adjustments downward from the strict outputs of Chart 9. Note that as inflation increases from very low rates the PE drops faster for higher growth rate stocks. This is why it was such a shock to own growth stocks from the late 1960's through the 1970's. Stocks with expected growth rates in the 15% to 20% or more range had dramatic PE corrections as the perceived world of very low inflation moved to a world of near 10% inflation.

There are different investment styles for different economic/market environments. The two primary styles we have discussed are the growth stock style and the value stock style. To reiterate, a growth stock is one whose earnings per share is growing at a rate meaningfully higher than that for the overall stock market, the dividend yield is generally lower than for the stock market and the price/earnings ratio can be two or more times the earnings growth rate. Ideally, the earnings growth will tend to be relatively stable and consistent over time.

The value stock style typically involves companies who are considered somewhat dull, are generally out-of-favor, sell at price/earnings ratios meaningfully below the overall stock market and usually have significant dividend yields (i.e., meaningfully higher than for the overall stock market). The value companies tend to have their stock prices determined by assets, net worth, value of natural resources and other balance sheet related items. An excellent rough formula to use for scouting out good value candidates is:

(Growth Rate of Earnings per Share + Dividend Yield) / PE

You want the resulting value from this equation to be as high as possible -- at least a value of 2 or more.

So, when you perceive that the economy is embarking on a long trend period of rising inflation (as in the early 1970's) you want to shift out of growth stock investing and move toward a value style emphasizing the above formula as a starting point. Of course, use of one simple formula does not negate the need to still do significant fundamental research on the stocks you purchase.

I want to stress that there is no magic formula for consistent success in equity investing. This is especially true over the short-term or even the intermediate-term. Still, the approach outlined above does utilize long-term empirical evidence to help one focus on the relationship of some key variables such as earnings growth rates, inflation, dividend yields and PE ratios. The average investor is bouncing off of the walls with no coherent approach to garnering long-term success. Still, good fundamental research on individual stocks is vital. Our goal is to help one focus energies on productive endeavors.

Stock Investing Fundamentals

Chart 1

Year	"VALUE" Windsor Fund	Windsor Index	"GROWTH" US Growth Fund	US Growth Index		Return/year
		1.000		1.000		
1959	16.4	1.164	29.9	1.299		
1960	11.2	1.294	63.1	2.119		
1961	29.6	1.678	35.6	2.873		Return/year
1962	-25.0	1.258	-21.5	2.255		
1963	12.7	1.418	32.4	2.986		
1964	13.9	1.615	36.6	4.079	Growth	18.4%
1965	29.1	2.085	19.7	4.882		
1966	-3.3	2.016	22.0	5.956	Value	10.2%
1967	31.5	2.651	36.2	8.113		
1968	21.4	3.219	4.1	8.445		
1969	-3.8	3.096	-5.4	7.989		
1970	6.4	3.294	-14.5	6.831		
1971	7.5	3.542	30.6	8.921		
1972	10.2	3.903	19.4	10.652		
1973	-25.0	2.927	-32.3	7.211		
1974	-16.8	2.435	-33.4	4.803		
1975	54.5	3.763	30.7	6.277		
1976	46.4	5.508	14.5	7.187		
1977	1.0	5.564	1.2	7.273		
1978	8.8	6.053	16.2	8.452		
1979	22.6	7.421	18.1	9.982	Growth	6.7%
1980	22.6	9.098	33.6	13.335		
1981	16.8	10.627	-0.5	13.269	Value	15.7%
1982	21.7	12.933	19.7	15.883		
1983	30.1	16.826	23.9	19.679		
1984	19.5	20.107	1.2	19.915		
1985	28.0	25.737	36.5	27.184		
1986	20.3	30.961	7.8	29.304		
1987	1.2	31.333	-6.1	27.516		
1988	28.7	40.325	8.8	29.938		
1989	15.0	46.374	37.7	41.224		
1990	-15.5	39.186	4.6	43.121		
1991	28.6	50.393	46.8	63.301		
1992	16.5	58.708	2.8	65.074		
1993	19.4	70.097	-1.5	64.097	Growth	21.3%
1994	-0.2	69.957	3.9	66.597		
1995	30.2	91.084	38.4	92.171	Value	13.2%
1996	26.4	115.130	26.1	116.227		
1997	22.0	140.459	25.9	146.330		
1998	0.8	141.582	40.0	204.862		
1999	11.6	158.006	22.3	250.546		
2000	15.9	183.129	-20.2	199.936		
2001	5.7	193.567	-31.7	136.556		
2002	-22.3	150.402	-35.8	87.669	Growth	-5.3%
2003	37.0	206.050	26.1	110.551		
2004	13.4	233.661	7.0	118.289	Value	4.6%
2005	5.0	245.344	11.2	131.538		
2006	19.4	292.941	1.8	133.905		
2007	-3.3	283.274	10.2	147.564		
2008	-41.1	166.848	-37.8	91.785		
2009	34.7	224.745	35.0	123.909		
2010	14.8	258.007	11.5	138.159		
		11.3% per year		9.9% per year		

Styles: Value vs. Growth

Chart 2

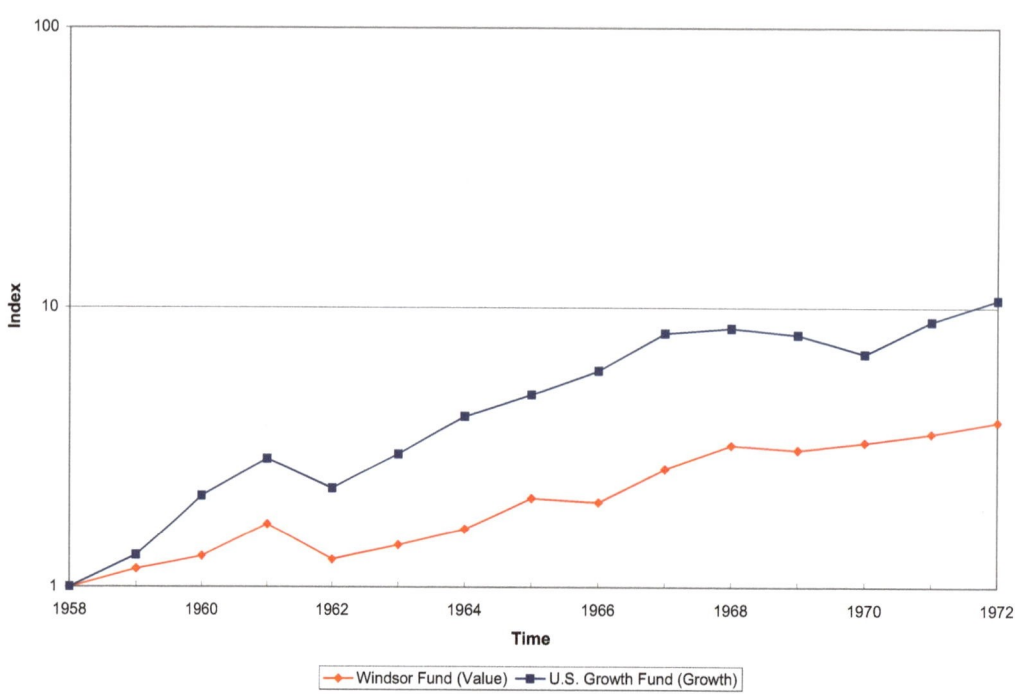

Windsor Fund (Value) — U.S. Growth Fund (Growth)

Styles: Value vs. Growth

Chart 3

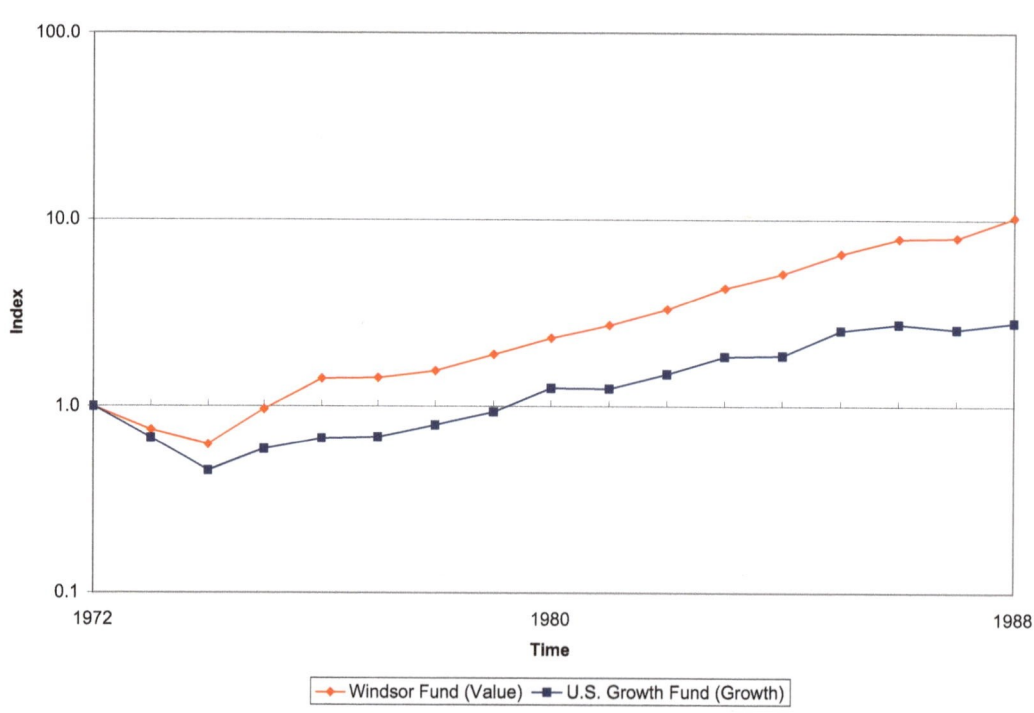

Windsor Fund (Value) — U.S. Growth Fund (Growth)

Styles: Value vs. Growth

Chart 4

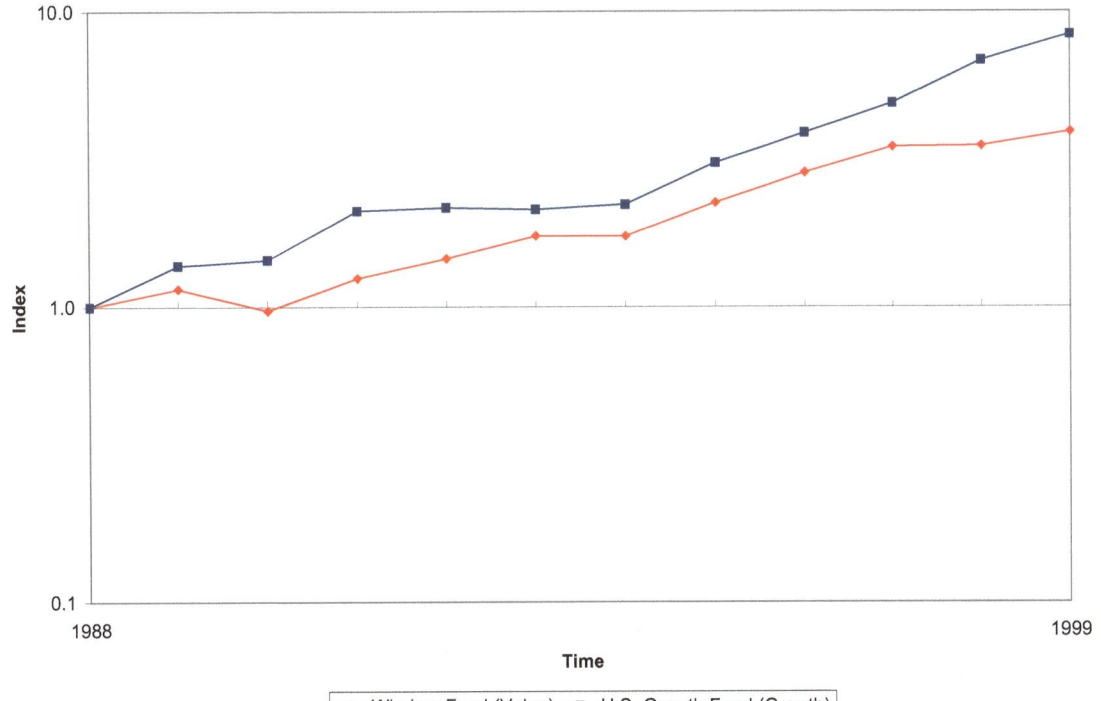

Styles: Value vs. Growth

Chart 5

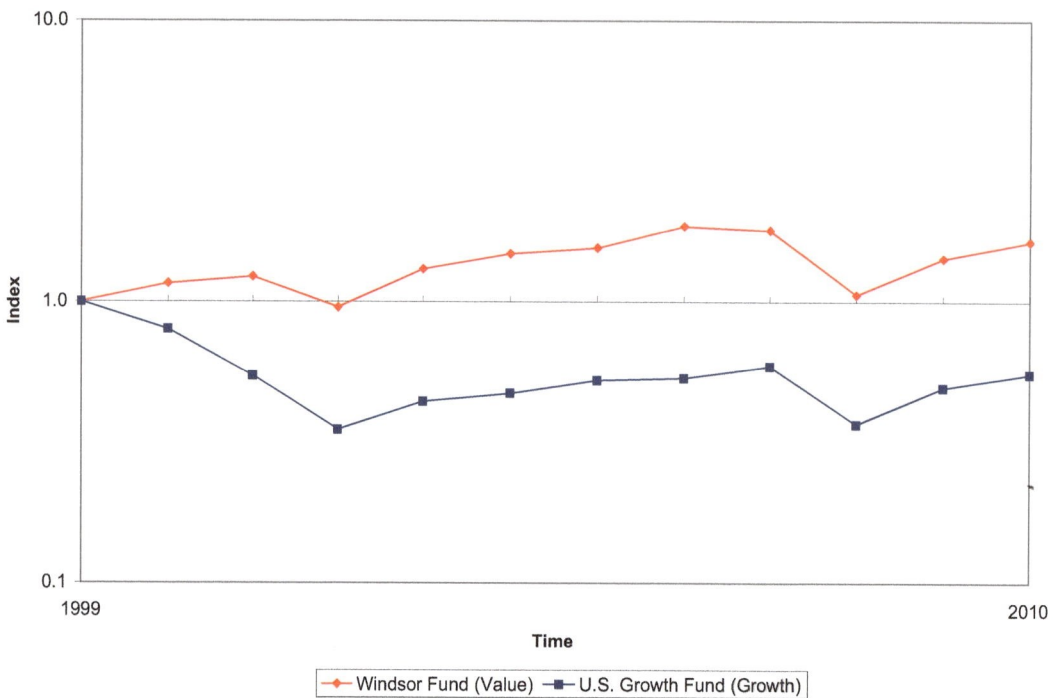

Styles: Value vs. Growth

Chart 6

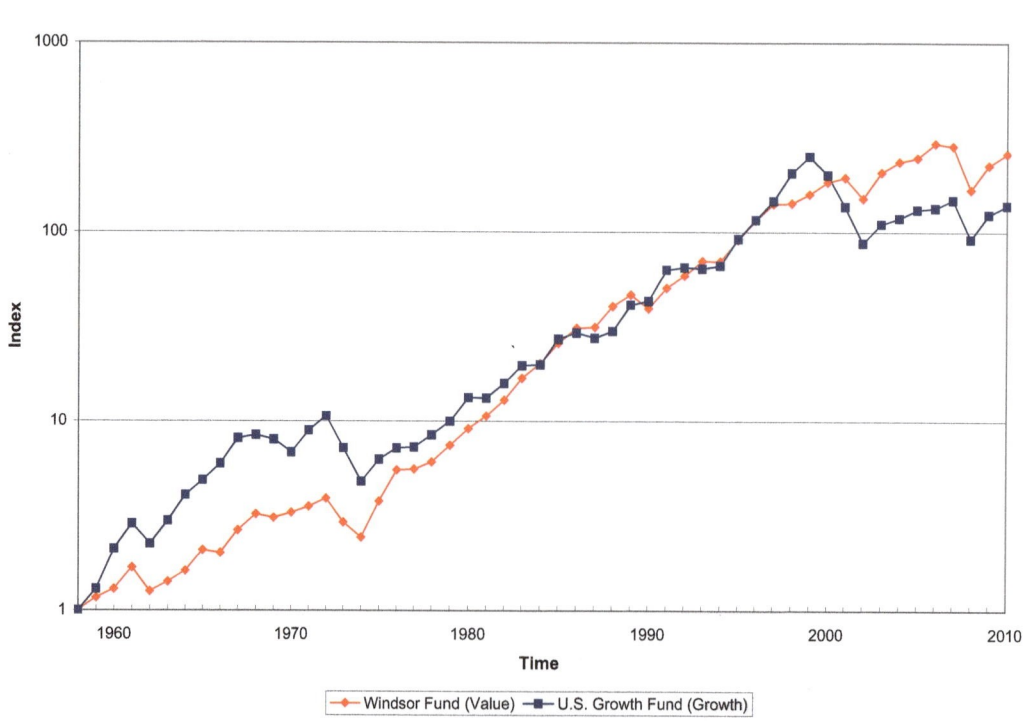

Styles: Growth vs. Value

Chart 7

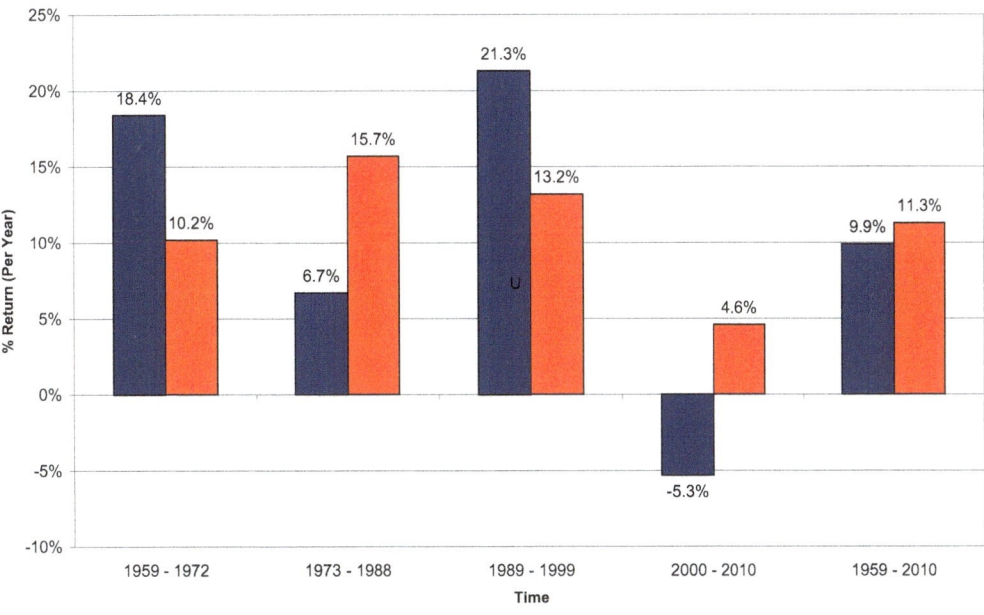

Chart 8

12/31/58 – 12/31/88

Average Annual Returns Over 30 Years

Windsor Fund   **13.1%/yr.**

U.S. Growth Fund   **12.0%/yr.**

Start With U.S. Growth, Move To Windsor:

12/31/69	**16.7%/yr.**
12/31/70	**15.9%/yr.**
12/31/71	**16.7%/yr.**
12/31/72	**17.0%/yr.**
12/31/73	**16.6%/yr.**
12/31/74	**15.7%/yr.**
12/31/75	**15.1%/yr.**

INFLATION	1 %		INFLATION	10 %
GROWTH	15 %		GROWTH	15 %

Chart 9

Year	EPS Growth 15%	PV		Year	EPS Growth 15%	PV
0	1.00	1.00		0	1.00	1.00
1	1.15	1.14		1	1.15	1.05
2	1.32	1.30		2	1.32	1.09
3	1.52	1.48		3	1.52	1.14
4	1.75	1.68		4	1.75	1.19
5	2.01	1.91		5	2.01	1.25
6	2.31	2.18		6	2.31	1.31
7	2.66	2.48		7	2.66	1.37
8	3.06	2.82		8	3.06	1.43
9	3.52	3.22		9	3.52	1.49
10	4.05	3.66		10	4.05	1.56
11	4.65	4.17		11	4.65	1.63
12	5.35	4.75		12	5.35	1.70
13	6.15	5.41		13	6.15	1.78
14	7.08	6.16		14	7.08	1.86
15	8.14	7.01		15	8.14	1.95
16	9.36	7.98		16	9.36	2.04
17	10.76	9.09		17	10.76	2.13
18	12.38	10.35		18	12.38	2.23
19	14.23	11.78		19	14.23	2.33
20	16.37	13.41		20	16.37	2.43

	PE	PE/g			PE	PE/g
5 Yrs.	7.51	0.50		5 Yrs.	5.72	0.38
6 Yrs.	9.68	0.65		6 Yrs.	7.03	0.47
7 Yrs.	12.17	0.81		7 Yrs.	8.40	0.56
8 Yrs.	14.99	1.00		8 Yrs.	9.82	0.65
9 Yrs.	18.21	1.21		9 Yrs.	11.31	0.75
10 Yrs.	21.87	1.46		10 Yrs.	12.87	0.86
11 Yrs.	26.04	1.74		11 Yrs.	14.50	0.97
12 Yrs.	30.79	2.05		12 Yrs.	16.21	1.08
13 Yrs.	36.19	2.41		13 Yrs.	17.99	1.20
14 Yrs.	42.35	2.82		14 Yrs.	19.85	1.32
15 Yrs.	49.36	3.29		15 Yrs.	21.80	1.45
16 Yrs.	57.34	3.82		16 Yrs.	23.84	1.59
17 Yrs.	66.43	4.43		17 Yrs.	25.97	1.73
18 Yrs.	76.77	5.12		18 Yrs.	28.19	1.88
19 Yrs.	88.55	5.90		19 Yrs.	30.52	2.03
20 Yrs.	101.96	6.80		20 Yrs.	32.95	2.20

Chart 10

30 YEAR INFLATION CYCLE

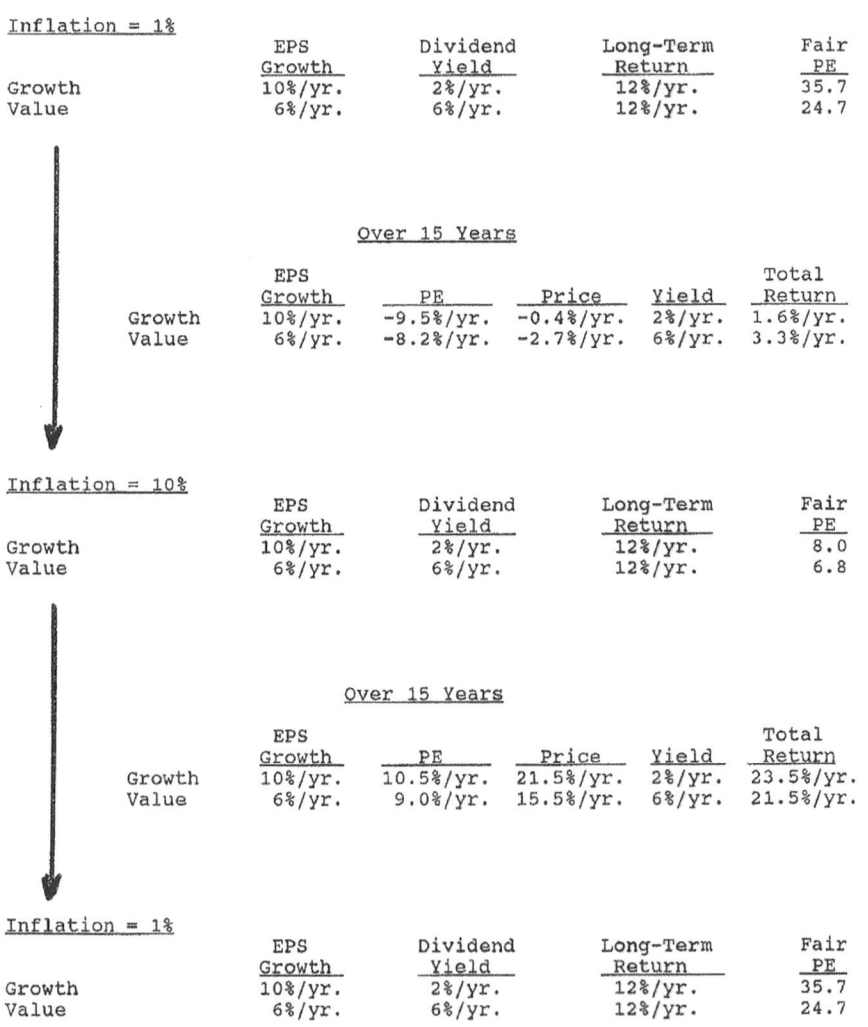

Inflation = 1%

	EPS Growth	Dividend Yield	Long-Term Return	Fair PE
Growth	10%/yr.	2%/yr.	12%/yr.	35.7
Value	6%/yr.	6%/yr.	12%/yr.	24.7

Over 15 Years

	EPS Growth	PE	Price	Yield	Total Return
Growth	10%/yr.	-9.5%/yr.	-0.4%/yr.	2%/yr.	1.6%/yr.
Value	6%/yr.	-8.2%/yr.	-2.7%/yr.	6%/yr.	3.3%/yr.

Inflation = 10%

	EPS Growth	Dividend Yield	Long-Term Return	Fair PE
Growth	10%/yr.	2%/yr.	12%/yr.	8.0
Value	6%/yr.	6%/yr.	12%/yr.	6.8

Over 15 Years

	EPS Growth	PE	Price	Yield	Total Return
Growth	10%/yr.	10.5%/yr.	21.5%/yr.	2%/yr.	23.5%/yr.
Value	6%/yr.	9.0%/yr.	15.5%/yr.	6%/yr.	21.5%/yr.

Inflation = 1%

	EPS Growth	Dividend Yield	Long-Term Return	Fair PE
Growth	10%/yr.	2%/yr.	12%/yr.	35.7
Value	6%/yr.	6%/yr.	12%/yr.	24.7

Eads & Heald Investment Counsel

PE vs. Inflation

Chart 11

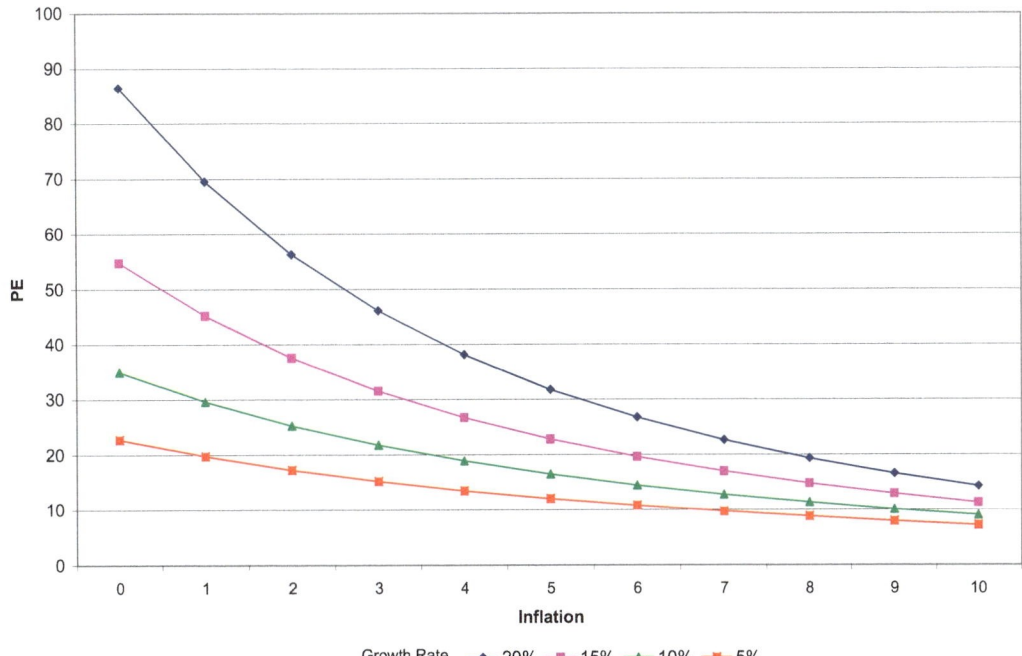

Chapter 15: Retirement Spending Model

Different people save to varying degrees for their retirement. Saving money is very difficult for most people simply because of the lack of enough money to do the things they need and/or want to do. A person finishes their education, gets a job, gets married, has children and so on. Between buying a house, furnishings, cars, food, utilities, vacations, schooling for the children, medical/dental and myriad other ongoing expenses there always seems to be something more important than saving. By the time the kids are all educated and one might start to seriously ponder retirement down the road the person might be in their mid-40's to mid-50's. Time is then limited to adequately save for retirement. These days, since the defined benefit pension plan is rare, many people are saving some money by way of a 401K-type plan at work. IRA's are also used to save. Even then, will the funds prove to be adequate at retirement?

We do not currently have a program to help people actually save money for retirement. Nor do we have a program to help them stop smoking or lose weight. All are very difficult endeavors. What we do is to provide a computer-based model for a person retiring, or just about to retire, to assist in gauging how much money can be spent in each year and still have adequate funds for the next 30 years. Our Retirement Spending Model can be found at this same Eads & Heald web site on the home page. It is free to use and we do not track any data entered or attempt to link it back to the user. Your privacy is protected.

See the model in Chart 1 below. We believe that the model is powerful for most users. However, for someone with extensive and/or exotic financial assets and income sources the model could well appear inadequate. When you first go to the model we suggest that you read our introductory briefing before actually jumping in to fill out the model inputs. After the introduction the model is designed to start inserting inputs without first having to complete a multi-page questionnaire which would be tedious and boring. Any inputs you make can be altered with a couple of keystrokes.

A vital input, which proves difficult for most people, is simply, "On retiring, how much money after federal and state income taxes will you need to spend in the first year to live your lifestyle?" Sounds simple….however, most people stumble coming up with an answer. After the first year the model will grow that number at the assumed rate of inflation for each following year. We recommend using 3.5% inflation. Again, the beauty of the model is that different scenarios can be tried instantly.

The model separates taxable funds from tax-sheltered funds for each of you and a spouse. Rate of return is broken up into two 15 year periods simply because the market does have a history of 30 year complete cycles which contain a good period and a not so good period. You should hope that the good returns come as soon as possible in the 30 year period. This is because your money will last longer than if the same good returns come later. You can assume your combined federal and state income tax rate….this is the overall rate and not just the highest marginal rate. There are provisions for entering Social Security benefits as well as defined benefit pension payments. If you are selling a business, you can enter the key factors of the sale. Also, if you have something like income from rental properties (or, whatever), enter that.

A computer-based model is only a guide. It is not a definitive answer to how your money will withstand the ravages of an unknown future. It will sort out the extreme possible outcomes of having more than adequate funds versus having totally inadequate funds. It is useful to be conservative in the inputs you use. For example, overstate inflation and the tax rate somewhat while you understate rates of return. Still, again, you can try myriad combinations of inputs. You will get a good feel for how sensitive the final outcome is to slight changes in a given input variable. The completed model on our web site is out of money in the 24th year. The couple would need to go back and review the model inputs along with their desired spending level. Even as an imperfect model it does give a means to consider alternatives and review spending in retirement.

The Retirement Spending Model below can be found and used interactively on our web site at http://www.EadsHeald.com.

Chart 1

This model is designed to be used by someone retired or within 3 years of retirement. The intent: gauge what realistic spending is possible given your resources. Delete the example entries in the boxes below, enter your data and click the "Update" button to view your results.

	SPOUSE	"YOU"		SPOUSE	"YOU"
Tax-Sheltered Funds When Model Begins (for Each):	75,000	175,000	SOCIAL SECURITY		
Joint Taxable Funds When Model Begins:		600,000	Current Age:	61	63
Total Funds When Model Begins:		850,000	Age to Start Social Security (62-70):	62	65
Funds Needed in Year 1 After Income Taxes (Current $'s Now):		75,000	Social Security in Start Year (Current $'s Now):	7,000	10,000
Inflation Rate - Percent:		3.0			

		PENSION	PENSION	BUYOUT	MISC
Return First 15 Years:	7.0	OTHER INCOME	SPOUSE	"YOU"	per "YOU"	per "YOU"
Return Second 15 Years:	5.0	Latter of Start Age or Now:	62	65	70	68
Overall Income Tax Rate (Combined Federal & State) - Percent:	34.0	# Yrs. to Run from This Age:	35	35	5	20
Latter of Retirement Age or Current Age for "YOU"(MODEL BEGINS)	65	Annual Income at This Age:	15,000	20,000	8,000	10,000
Current Age for "YOU":	63	COLA (%/year):	1	1	0	2

Year	Tax Sheltered Funds	Taxable Funds	Total Funds	Need After Tax	P/T Funds Needed + w/d Taxable Funds	Social Security P/T	Pension & Buyout & Misc. Income P/T	Mandatory w/d Tax Sheltered Funds P/T	Elective w/d Tax Sheltered Funds P/T	Total w/d Tax Sheltered Funds P/T	w/d(d/p) Taxable Funds	Total Funds Adj. for Inflation
0	250,000	600,000	850,000									850,000
1	267,500	583,255	850,755	79,568	97,651	18,035	35,150	0	0	0	44,465	825,976
2	286,225	563,938	850,163	81,955	100,341	18,576	35,502	0	0	0	46,263	801,360
3	306,261	541,872	848,133	84,413	103,110	19,134	35,857	0	0	0	48,120	776,162
4	327,699	523,470	851,169	86,946	109,359	19,708	46,215	0	0	0	43,437	756,253
5	350,638	502,371	853,009	89,554	112,360	20,299	46,777	0	0	0	45,284	735,813
6	366,225	489,580	855,805	92,241	121,213	20,908	55,347	8,958	0	8,958	36,000	716,723
7	382,288	474,632	856,920	95,008	124,599	21,535	55,925	9,572	0	9,572	37,567	696,755
8	394,424	460,290	854,714	97,858	129,585	22,181	56,510	14,624	0	14,624	36,270	674,719
9	406,407	443,842	850,250	100,794	133,290	22,847	57,103	15,626	0	15,626	37,714	651,646
10	418,160	425,166	843,326	103,818	137,115	23,532	57,705	16,696	0	16,696	39,182	627,513
11	429,592	398,855	828,447	106,932	138,345	24,238	50,314	17,839	0	17,839	45,954	598,488
12	440,605	369,812	810,418	110,140	142,425	24,965	50,932	19,058	0	19,058	47,469	568,411
13	451,155	337,846	789,002	113,444	146,616	25,714	51,559	20,292	0	20,292	49,051	537,272
14	461,060	302,842	763,902	116,848	150,969	26,485	52,194	21,677	0	21,677	50,613	505,029
15	470,296	264,564	734,859	120,353	155,426	27,280	52,838	23,038	0	23,038	52,270	471,678
16	469,297	219,359	688,655	123,964	160,039	28,098	53,490	24,514	0	24,514	53,936	429,147
17	467,235	170,604	637,839	127,682	164,613	28,941	54,152	25,526	0	25,526	55,994	385,903
18	464,027	118,114	582,142	131,513	169,322	29,810	54,823	26,570	0	26,570	58,119	341,947
19	459,584	61,696	521,280	135,458	174,168	30,704	55,503	27,644	0	27,644	60,316	297,279
20	453,814	1,144	454,958	139,522	179,155	31,625	56,193	28,749	0	28,749	62,588	251,899
21	350,022	0	350,022	143,708	217,130	32,574	56,892	29,743	96,740	126,482	1,182	188,154
22	234,404	0	234,404	148,019	224,271	33,551	57,601	23,887	109,232	133,119	0	122,334
23	108,003	0	108,003	152,460	230,999	34,557	58,320	16,475	121,647	138,122	0	54,724
24	0	0	0	157,033	237,929	35,594	44,189	10,048	103,354	113,403	0	0
25	0	0	0	161,744	245,067	36,662	44,631	0	0	0	0	0
26	0	0	0	166,597	252,419	37,762	45,077	0	0	0	0	0
27	0	0	0	171,595	259,992	38,895	45,528	0	0	0	0	0
28	0	0	0	176,742	267,792	40,062	45,984	0	0	0	0	0
29	0	0	0	182,045	275,825	41,263	46,443	0	0	0	0	0
30	0	0	0	187,506	284,100	42,501	46,908	0	0	0	0	0

Click here to read important notes about the model.

Chapter 16: Who Can Best Assist you with Your Investment Needs and How Should They Be Compensated?

Years ago there was an actor/comedian named Jimmy Durante who often noted that "everyone wants to get into the act". This has become very true regarding the business of managing money for people. Today, in addition to traditional stock brokers and banks, there is now an array of money managers from the insurance industry, certified public accounting, estate planning, mutual fund industry, independent investment advisors and so on. There are long television infomercials selling you the opportunity to manage your own stock portfolios with the easy buy/sell trading secrets they will teach you. They teach you how to consistently buy low and sell high. This type pitch no doubt appeals to the more gullible consumer who can least afford to lose money.

So, what is one to do? Well, you can't go wrong using an investment firm that advertises on, say, the Super Bowl……can you? To be that rich and well known they must have been doing something right. True, but something right for who…themselves or the customer? Toss in the fact that myriad scamsters have emerged over the past few years who were managing money for people until the money all evaporated. There is a fine line between a crook and a firm that is not a crook but still puts their interests before the customer's interest.

Eads & Heald started in 1987. In our formative days we acquired much of our business from brokerage firms who wanted to gather assets but not actually manage the money themselves. Or, at least, their brokers had the latitude to use outside money managers. One such stockbroker was with a very large, well known national firm and had referred a couple of large clients to us. However, although we were producing very good results for these clients, no other referrals were coming from this broker. Once we called the broker to inquire about this and we were told that while we had the best investment results of all of the outside money managers he was using we simply did not trade securities enough to create a lot of commissions. In other words, investment results aside, this broker was placing clients with outside firms that created a lot of commissions for him. While this is obviously not surprising it is nonetheless troubling that the client well being was not the first priority. Eads & Heald always puts client interests first. Unfortunately, that has not been how all of Wall Street has conducted business over the years.

One good place to start might be to look for a firm that has as its sole business managing money in securities. This is not to rule out, say, real estate investments. However, while real estate can be an excellent income producing investment it can also be much less liquid than stocks or bonds if you need to sell it. In addition, it requires a very different skill set to evaluate real estate than, say, stocks or bonds. The point is that when your investment firm is in a multitude of businesses such as banking, insurance, annuities, estate planning, etc. you may be fair game to sell some of the other products that simply need to be sold. This could be due to higher profit margins in other products, shore up a lagging division within the overall company or maybe to help you. You simply never know.

How about the fee? It would seem that the best way to charge a fee is to have it based on a percent of the assets under management. This way the money manager has a real incentive to see the assets grow. This could be by way of more deposits from the happy client or because the assets grew on their own merit. Should the client be concerned that the money manager might take reckless risks to make the assets grow very fast? That would be a silly way to run a proper business. That type manager would be screened out in the initial decision selection process. Factors such as length of time in business, investment results, credentials regarding employers and education, client references and like items would be used to only consider experienced, ethical money managers.

The international gold standard in credentials for a money manager is being a Chartered Financial Analyst. This requires a certain level of work experience in addition to three exhaustive all day exams on all facets of analyzing securities. The exams are generally taken some months apart. Also, the highest possible standards of ethics are monitored and enforced. If the money manager does not have the Chartered Financial Analyst designation, you should ask why not. Scamsters tend to not have these credentials. They seek out the "easier road" to make money.

Chapter 17: Future Investment Themes

Forecasting future investment themes can be a valuable exercise to assist you in achieving long-term investment success. As implied earlier, it is good to have as many things as possible supporting the fundamentals of the securities you purchase.

We define a Future Theme as an unfolding story that gives a dramatic boost to certain stocks over, say, at least a five year period of time. Another way to understand this idea is to look backward. That is, pick out some very successful stocks over the past five years. Then, ask yourself if there were any important themes that helped to propel any of these stocks to stardom. You could attempt to list as bullet items on one 8 ½ x 11 piece of paper trends that you believe could possibly have a dramatic effect on certain sectors of investing over the next five years. Better yet, form a small group that meets to define, and periodically refine, such a list.

It should be admitted that while this is an extremely fun task it is not an easy one. While is seems easy to blue sky some ideas they may turn out to be a bust so far as attaching stocks to the ideas. Also, a good theme can easily go a mere five years remaining totally unfulfilled. Ideas such as such as the extreme importance of plentiful water for the cities or reaping a bounty from the oceans are two past themes largely stillborn in so far as success in the stock market.

Let's go back to the introduction of the Interstate Highway system in the U.S. One theme might have been to forecast the springing up of successful chains of moderately priced restaurants and lodging (not traditional city hotels nor like the old motels on the two lane highways). Think of names like Cracker Barrel and Hampton Inn (Hilton). Ideally, a theme would be a "gimme" so far as it was destined to happen. Then, the catch would be to find stocks that could ride the theme to success.

Hindsight is always easy. When you look back at companies that achieved great success there might have been dozens of companies vying for that success at the outset. The new wave of discount mass merchandising allowed Wal-Mart to pick up the pace and sort of take over and do it better than K-Mart. Home Depot rode the DIY (Do It Yourself) boom and consolidated places like the local hardware store, lumber store, appliance, Handy City type stores and myriad others into one big orange box. Home Depot was joined by a redefined Lowes. Best Buy big boxed electronics retailing. In the late 1960's and on Intel rode the next wave of electronics miniaturization into integrated circuitry. The advent of the personal computer helped propel that wave. Never forget that early in the last century there were many U.S. automobile companies that later distilled down to mainly General Motors, Ford and Chrysler. Haloid Corporation (Xerox) had many challengers at the outset of copying. Years later, Xerox was redefining and fighting for its existence. At one time the Polaroid (instant self developing) camera was great innovative technology. However Kodak and film still had a place to exist for a period of time. Digital cameras have the film camera world on end. Themes, themes, themes.......what are the great future themes?

It is great fun to search out Future Themes. However, good themes are difficult to locate and it is even more difficult to align good public companies with the themes. Below are a few themes we cite to get you thinking. Good luck!

A SAMPLING OF OUR FUTURE THEMES

➢ The last calendar decade has been the worst decade for the NYSE markets in history. The law of "mean reversion" would seem to indicate that the next decade would be witness to a positive long-term trend in equity returns.

➢ The U.S. economy appears to be stagnant, possibly because we are at a pivotal economic and political crossroads. This presents a thick layer of uncertainty to investors, which the market greatly dislikes. A reduction in this level of uncertainty combined with low interest rates, low inflation, and improving earnings would bode well for stocks.

➢ Inflation will stay moderate for now. However, seeds are being sown for the next round of upward pressure on inflation.

➢ Tax rates will rise as it becomes increasingly apparent that revenues will not be sufficient to meet future obligations. The Government faces increased public debt as a percent of GDP.

➢ A renewed focus on American politics has shifted attention away from economic and investment fundamentals for the time being. This trend will continue at least through the next election cycle.

➢ The steady increase in the U.S. standard of living is not guaranteed over the next decade. The U.S. will face greater international competition for global economic leadership.

➢ The U.S. will be forced to refocus massive efforts on renovating the educational system as emerging countries press ahead with better scores, especially in the areas of math and science. Failure to do so will further erode the U.S. position in the global economy.

➢ In the wake of the "great recession", savings rates will trend along at levels higher than seen before the recession. The breadth and depth of the recession have likely etched a long-lasting scar into the minds of many, as the great depression did to another generation.

➢ Demographics will continue to point toward an aging population. An aging population will require an increasingly large portion of the federal budget devoted to funding entitlement programs.

➢ Those industries which face relatively less Federal regulation may prove to be more attractive investment opportunities. Federal over-regulation tends to stifle performance.

➢ After years of intense and successful competition from international automakers combined with the recent threat of domestic automaker collapse, some U.S. automakers will continue to show a renewed vigor in designing and selling cars. Ford especially is making a bold statement with its financial position and new car development.

➢ There is potentially more trouble to come on the housing front. A backlog of foreclosures in the system, combined with a large shadow inventory and a rising trend toward strategic defaults, will likely put additional pressure on the housing market.

➢ While the internet will continue to have profound effects on the transmission of information, it will continue to become yet another utility like the telephone or electricity.

➢ Personal computer and technology advancements will open up even greater use within the home and office. More routine functions will be handled by computer software, hardware, simple microchips and barcodes.

➢ Cloud computing will continue to evolve and gain greater acceptance. Adoption will be slowed somewhat by fears over privacy and security for critical applications.

➢ The networked home will become ubiquitous. Just as every home once had a VCR and currently has a DVD player and personal computer, every home will be networked for home entertainment. Sharing of files, photos, videos, etc. will be facilitated by a central "hub".

➢ Faster data connections, mobile computing and networked homes are changing the media landscape. Electronic versions of books, music and movies are replacing the physical media.

➢ Demand for data storage will grow as all sorts of data and files are stored in electronic format.

➢ Healthcare will continue in transition as the federal government implements insurance exchanges and other elements of the health care bill. Additionally, the continued rise in drug prices, the threat of drug price controls and the price benefits of generic drug competition will become pivotal issues.

➢ Biotechnology/genetic engineering will continue to make exciting progress in the years ahead as more and more secrets about the human body and disease are uncovered. The potential medical benefits versus the controversial nature of the research will continue to be the subject of heated political debate.

➢ The move toward a one-world/international economy will continue at a solid pace as economic borders continue to shrink. Economic problems around the world will affect the U.S. economy to a troubling extent.

➢ China will continue to move toward capitalism and maintain a reputation as an economic powerhouse. This, combined with the innate Chinese work ethic, will have far-reaching effects around the world with the scope difficult to foresee.

➢ India will challenge China's leadership position among developing countries. Economic liberalization and reform over the past 15 years will begin to bear fruit.

➢ The ever increasing trade deficit will be difficult to reverse if China remains steadfast in pegging their currency to the dollar and other parts of the globe continue to experience slow economic growth (Europe).

➢ Russia appears to be reasserting power and should continue to grow and establish itself in the world economy. However, the move toward a free and efficient economy may be slow. It will take many more years to see dramatic progress in the overall standard of living, but progress is evident.

➢ Terrorism is a permanent fixture in America. While we can work to reduce the risks of major attacks, well organized terrorist groups or individuals will always find a way to inflict damage. Terrorist attacks and the corresponding U.S. response may shock the market temporarily.

➢ Retailing will continue a trend toward no frills and low pricing. Low-priced retailing combined with fashionable trends and products will be a popular formula.

➢ We will continue to move toward a cashless/checkless society.

Chapter 18: About The Author

R. Stewart Eads, President, is a CFA (Chartered Financial Analyst) charterholder and has an MBA degree from the Wharton Graduate School at the University of Pennsylvania along with bachelors and masters degrees in Electrical Engineering from the Georgia Institute of Technology. He has furthered his investment training at Stanford University and the University of Chicago in addition to other ongoing continuing education.

Mr. Eads spent 15 years in the Atlanta office of the Boston-based investment management firm of Thorndike, Doran, Paine and Lewis/Wellington Management Company where he served as Vice President, Senior Portfolio Manager and analyst. At Wellington, Mr. Eads managed accounts for clients such as Duke Power Company, Sherwin-Williams, City of Savannah, GA, Chatham County, GA, Emerson Electric, Trane, Annuity Board of the Southern Baptist Convention, E-Systems, St. Mary's University, Sheet Metal Workers, University of Alabama Endowment, The Citadel Endowment, etc. His accounts totaled over $300 million.

In addition to serving as a portfolio manager, his other major contributions included establishing a system for setting client investment objectives, founding and chairing the Future Themes Group that forecasts major trends in the economy and society that have investment significance over five years, and deriving a methodology to determine secular shifts in equity valuation (i.e., price/earnings ratios).

Prior to joining Thorndike/Wellington, Mr. Eads was an investment analyst with The Hartford Insurance Group for three years. Overall, he has been an investment professional for 43 years.

Mr. Eads' initial employment after receiving his MBA degree was in the Office of the Director at the U.S. Central Intelligence Agency. Also, he spent time working with NASA on the moon project under Dr. Wernher von Braun.

www.ingramcontent.com/pod-product-compliance
Lightning Source LLC
Chambersburg PA
CBHW050751180526
45159CB00003B/1425